THE PREHISTORIC EARTH

EARLY HUMANS

THE PLEISTOCENE & HOLOCENE EPOCHS

THE PREHISTORIC EARTH

Early Life:
The Cambrian Period

The First Vertebrates:
Oceans of the Paleozoic Era

March Onto Land:
The Silurian Period to the Middle Triassic Epoch

Dawn of the Dinosaur Age:
The Late Triassic & Early Jurassic Epochs

Time of the Giants:
The Middle & Late Jurassic Epochs

Last of the Dinosaurs:
The Cretaceous Period

The Rise of Mammals:
The Paleocene & Eocene Epochs

The Age of Mammals:
The Oligocene & Miocene Epochs

Primates and Human Ancestors:
The Pliocene Epoch

Early Humans:
The Pleistocene & Holocene Epochs

THE PREHISTORIC EARTH

EARLY HUMANS

THE PLEISTOCENE & HOLOCENE EPOCHS

Thom Holmes

CHELSEA HOUSE
PUBLISHERS

An imprint of Infobase Publishing

THE PREHISTORIC EARTH: Early Humans

Copyright © 2009 by Infobase Publishing

Chelsea House
An imprint of Infobase Publishing
132 West 31st Street
New York NY 10001

Library of Congress Cataloging-in-Publication Data

Holmes, Thom.
  Early humans : the Pleistocene & Holocene epochs / by Thom Holmes.
    p. cm. — (The prehistoric earth)
  Includes bibliographical references and index.
  ISBN 978-0-8160-5966-9 (hardcover)
  1. Fossil hominids. 2. Human evolution. 3. Pleistocene-Holocene boundary. I. Title. II. Series.

  GN282.H638 2009
  569.9—dc22   2008038936

Chelsea House books are available at special discounts when purchased in bulk quantities for businesses, associations, institutions, or sales promotions. Please call our Special Sales Department in New York at (212) 967-8800 or (800) 322-8755.

You can find Chelsea House on the World Wide Web at http://www.chelseahouse.com

Text design by Kerry Casey
Cover design by Salvatore Luongo
Section opener images © John Sibbick

Printed in the United States of America

Bang NMSG 10 9 8 7 6 5 4 3 2 1

This book is printed on acid-free paper.

All links and Web addresses were checked and verified to be correct at the time of publication. Because of the dynamic nature of the Web, some addresses and links may have changed since publication and may no longer be valid.

CONTENTS

PREFACE

To be curious about the future one must know something about the past.

Humans have been recording events in the world around them for about 5,300 years. That is how long it has been since the Sumerian people, in a land that is today part of southern Iraq, invented the first known written language. Writing allowed people to document what they saw happening around them. The written word gave a new permanency to life. Language, and writing in particular, made history possible.

History is a marvelous human invention, but how do people know about things that happened before language existed? Or before humans existed? Events that took place before human record keeping began are called *prehistory*. Prehistoric life is, by its definition, any life that existed before human beings existed and were able to record for posterity what was happening in the world around them.

Prehistory is as much a product of the human mind as history. Scientists who specialize in unraveling clues of prehistoric life are called *paleontologists*. They study life that existed before human history, often hundreds of thousands and millions, and even billions, of years in the past. Their primary clues come from fossils of animals, plants, and other organisms, as well as from geologic evidence about Earth's topography and climate. Through the skilled and often clever interpretation of fossils, paleontologists are able to reconstruct the appearances, lifestyles, environments, and relationships of ancient life forms. While paleontology is grounded in a study of prehistoric life, it draws on many other sciences to complete an accurate picture of the past. Information from the fields of biology, zoology, geology, chemistry, meteorology, and even astrophysics is called into play to help the paleontologist view the past through the lens of today's knowledge.

If a writer were to write a history of all sports, would it be enough to write only about table tennis? Certainly not. On the shelves of bookstores and libraries, however, we find just such a slanted perspective toward the story of the dinosaurs. Dinosaurs have captured our imagination at the expense of many other equally fascinating, terrifying, and unusual creatures. Dinosaurs were not alone in the pantheon of prehistoric life, but it is rare to find a book that also mentions the many other kinds of life that came before and after the dinosaurs.

The Prehistoric Earth is a series that explores the evolution of life from its earliest forms 3.5 billion years ago until the emergence of modern humans about 200,000 years ago. Three volumes in the series trace the story of the dinosaurs. Seven other volumes are devoted to the kinds of animals that evolved before, during, and after the reign of the dinosaurs. *The Prehistoric Earth* covers the early explosion of life in the oceans; the invasion of the land by the first land animals; the rise of fishes, amphibians, reptiles, mammals, and birds; and the emergence of modern humans.

The Prehistoric Earth series is written for readers in middle school and high school. Based on the latest scientific findings in paleontology, *The Prehistoric Earth* is the most comprehensive and up-to-date series of its kind for this age group.

The first volume in the series, *Early Life*, offers foundational information about geologic time, Earth science, fossils, the classification of organisms, and evolution. This volume also begins the chronological exploration of fossil life that explodes with the incredible life-forms of the Precambrian and Cambrian Periods, more than 500 million years ago.

The remaining nine volumes in the series can be read chronologically. Each volume covers a specific geologic time period and describes the major forms of life that lived at that time. The books also trace the geologic forces and climate changes that affected the evolution of life through the ages. Readers of *The Prehistoric Earth* will see the whole picture of prehistoric life take shape. They will learn about forces that affect life on Earth, the directions that life can sometimes take, and ways in which all life-forms depend on each other in the environment. Along the way, readers also will meet many of the scientists who have made remarkable discoveries about the prehistoric Earth.

The language of science is used throughout this series, with ample definition and with an extensive glossary provided in each volume. Important concepts involving geology, evolution, and the lives of early animals are presented logically, step by step. Illustrations, photographs, tables, and maps reinforce and enhance the books' presentation of the story of prehistoric life.

While telling the story of prehistoric life, the author hopes that many readers will be sufficiently intrigued to continue studies on their own. For this purpose, throughout each volume, special "Think About It" sidebars offer additional insights or interesting exercises for readers who wish to explore certain topics. Each book in the series also provides a chapter-by-chapter bibliography of books, journals, and Web sites.

Only about one-tenth of 1 percent of all species of prehistoric animals are known from fossils. A multitude of discoveries remain to be made in the field of paleontology. It is with earnest, best wishes that I hope that some of these discoveries will be made by readers inspired by this series.

—Thom Holmes
Jersey City, New Jersey

ACKNOWLEDGMENTS

I want to thank the many dedicated and hardworking people at Chelsea House and Facts on File, some of whom I know but many of whom work behind the scenes. A special debt of gratitude goes to my editors—Frank Darmstadt, Brian Belval, Shirley White, Lisa Rand, and Justine Ciovacco—for their support and guidance in conceiving and making *The Prehistoric Earth* a reality. Frank and Brian were instrumental in fine-tuning the features of the series as well as accepting my ambitious plan for creating a comprehensive reference for students. Brian greatly influenced input during production. Shirley's excellent questions about the science behind the books contributed greatly to the readability of the result. The excellent copyediting of Mary Ellen Kelly was both thoughtful and vital to shaping the final manuscript. I thank Mary Ellen for her patience as well as her valuable review and suggestions that help make the books a success.

The most important collaborators on a series like this are the scientific consultants who lend their time to fact-check and advise the author. I am privileged to work with some of the brightest minds in paleoanthropology on this series. Dr. Conrad Phillip Kottak, professor of anthropology at the University of Michigan, reviewed the draft of *Early Humans* and made many important suggestions that affected the course of the work. Conrad served as the chair of the anthropology department at the University of Michigan from 1996 to 2006, leading one of the most prestigious programs in the country. His work and those of his University of Michigan colleagues including biologist Richard D. Alexander and paleoanthropologist Milford H. Wolpoff figure importantly in telling the story of early human evolution. Conrad also wrote the Foreword for the volume.

Breathing life into prehistoric creatures is also the work of natural history artists, many of whom have contributed to this series.

I especially want to thank John Sibbick, a major contributor to the artwork seen in *The Prehistoric Earth*. John's work is renowned among paleontologists, many of whom he has worked with side by side.

In many ways, a set of books such as this requires years of preparation. Some of the work is educational, and I owe much gratitude to Dr. Peter Dodson of the University of Pennsylvania for his gracious and inspiring tutelage over the years. I also thank Dr. William B. Gallagher of the New Jersey State Museum for both lessons learned in the classroom and in the historic fossil beds of New Jersey. Another dimension of preparation requires experience digging fossils, and for giving me these opportunities I thank my friends and colleagues who have taken me into the field with them, including Phil Currie, Rodolfo Coria, Matthew Lammana, Josh Smith, and Rubén Martínez.

Finally comes the work needed to put thoughts down on paper and complete the draft of a book, a process that always takes many more hours than I plan on. I thank Anne for bearing with my constant state of busy-ness, jokes about jawless fishes, and penguin notes, and for helping me remember the important things in life. You are an inspiration to me. I also thank my daughter, Shaina, the true genius in the family and another constant inspiration, for always being supportive and humoring her dad's obsession with prehistoric life, even as he becomes part of it.

FOREWORD

Thom Holmes's series of books, *The Prehistoric Earth,* of which this is the tenth and final volume, is written for middle and high school students. It provides a readable and comprehensive introduction to evolutionary thought and theory and to the principles and mechanisms of evolution and genetics developed to explain the origin and diversity of life on Earth, from the earliest organisms to anatomically modern humans and our nearest relatives, nonhuman primates.

This volume, *Early Humans: The Pleistocene & Holocene Epochs,* focuses on ancient and more modern members of the genus *Homo,* which today is represented by a single species, *Homo sapiens*—anatomically modern humans—that have been on this planet some 200,000 years. Book 10 describes the evolutionary development of human anatomy and culture over the past 2 million years. Book 9 of the series examines the beginning of that history, including the divergence (between 7 million and 5 million years ago) of early members of the human line (hominins) from the lines leading to gorillas and chimpanzees, our nearest relatives. In both books we meet the first hominins living in Africa around 5 million years ago. Book 9 described the first 3 million years of hominin evolution. Book 10 tells the last 2 million years of the story.

Here we meet *Homo habilis,* the first member of our genus, then later members, including early *Homo erectus,* sometimes called *Homo ergaster.* We learn how *Homo erectus* managed to extend the human range beyond Africa, to Asia and Europe, and we meet the successors of *Homo erectus* in Europe, Asia, and Africa. Among those successors were *Homo antecessor,* known from Spain, and *Homo heidelbergensis,* with a much wider distribution, including Europe, Asia, and Africa. Described throughout this book are the key anatomical changes, as well as the cultural advances, associated with different branches of the hominin line. The last half million years witnessed the appearance of the Neandertals in Europe and the Middle East, and of early *Homo sapiens* in, then spreading out of, Africa. Described here are the physical and cultural characteristics of both groups, and how those traits figured in their adaptations to environmental challenges, including those of the Ice Ages. This is a fascinating story of human origins and expansion, of our ancestors and evolution, including the eventual spread of *Homo sapiens* from the Old World into Australia and the Americas.

The story of human origins and evolution is intrinsically interesting, and Holmes does his best to convey the excitement of the field to his intended audience. Remembering my own teen years in public schools, I wish such a series as *The Prehistoric Earth* had existed then. I might have been hooked on a career in paleontology or anthropology even sooner. As it was, I had to wait for college for my introduction to those fields. Knowledge of human evolution has advanced tremendously since those days, and public schools actually have become more tolerant of evolution than when I attended junior high and high school. I hope this series and this volume find the large, attentive, and appreciative audience they deserve.

—Conrad Phillip Kottak
University of Michigan
National Academy of Sciences of the United States

INTRODUCTION

With this volume, *Early Humans*, the series *The Prehistoric Earth* concludes its journey through the **evolution** of vertebrate life. The focus of this volume is **anthropology**, the academic discipline that encompasses the study of biological and cultural human evolution. *Early Humans* continues the story of human biological evolution while introducing several other specialties in anthropological study such as the evolution of language, **culture**, and societies.

Anthropologist Michael Alan Park of Central Connecticut State University characterizes the field of anthropology as the "holistic study of the human **species**." The study is holistic, he explains, because it is a discipline of research that "assumes an interrelationship among its parts." The biological history of humans is related to the cultural history of humans. The human past is related to the human present.

I am most fortunate to have anthropologist Conrad Kottak as scientific consultant on this volume. Conrad has taught me that when you begin to look closely into the evolution of humans, you are compelled to see beyond the mere study of **fossil** bones and teeth to the qualities that make us who we are: a diversity of races, cultures, and beliefs, with the will to dream about the future and all of its possibilities. "Anthropology is a humanistic science devoted to discovering, describing, and explaining similarities and differences in time and space," writes Conrad.

This holistic approach to the study of human evolution has been an underlying goal in the writing of *Early Humans*. This volume concludes the story of premodern **hominin** evolution that was begun in *Primates and Human Ancestors*. It then continues by exploring the nature of **anatomically modern humans**, their origins, and their development, both biological and cultural.

OVERVIEW OF *EARLY HUMANS*

Early Humans is divided into two sections. Section One, "The Rise of Modern Humans," discusses the trends in hominin evolution that led to modern humans. Chapter 1, "Early Hominins and the Emergence of the Genus *Homo*," explores the emergence, by the end of the Pliocene Epoch, of the **genus** *Homo* as a species distinct from other early hominins. The chapter also looks at the best known species of early hominins, including *Australopithecus*, from Africa.

Chapter 2, "Archaic *Homo* Species," traces the discoveries of early *Homo*, describes key specimens, and discusses problems of establishing evolutionary links between modern *Homo* and ancestral humans.

Section Two, "Modern Humans," encompasses the rise of anatomically modern humans, otherwise known as **Homo sapiens**. Chapter 3, "Premodern Humans of the Genus *Homo*," examines the most recent *Homo* species to emerge during the past 500,000 years, just prior to the rise of modern humans in the form of *Homo sapiens*. Among these now-lost human species are the *H. neanderthalensis*, or Neandertals, the best known early peoples other than *H. sapiens*, as well as *H. heidelbergensis* from Germany and *H. floresiensis* from Indonesia, the recently discovered so-called "hobbit" species.

Chapter 4, "The Emergence of Modern Humans—Homo sapiens," concludes *Early Humans* with a close look at our own species. The chapter explores the emergence of *Homo sapiens*, their biology, their geographic radiation, and aspects of their early culture that laid the foundation for their longevity as the only surviving species of the *Homo* **taxon** today.

As with all volumes of *The Prehistoric Earth*, the discussion in *Early Humans* is governed always by the underlying principles that guide evolution: that the process of evolution is set in motion first by the traits inherited by individuals and then by the interaction of a **population** of a species with those traits with its habitat. As Charles Darwin (1809–1882) explained, "The small differences distinguishing varieties of the same species steadily tend to increase, till they equal the greater differences between species of the same genus, or even of distinct genera." These are the rules of nature that continually stoke the engine of evolution, giving rise to forms of life whose descendants still populate Earth.

SECTION ONE:
THE RISE OF
MODERN HUMANS

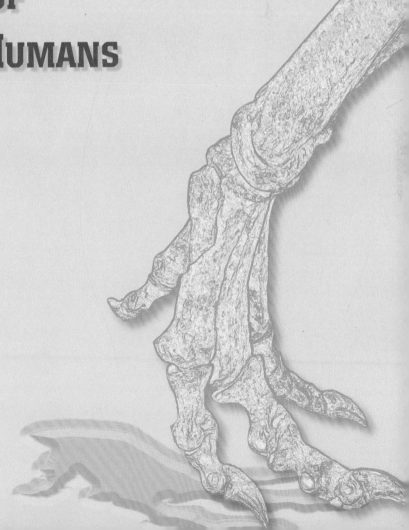

EARLY HOMININS AND THE EMERGENCE OF THE GENUS *HOMO*

Humans stand today not as the apex of an evolutionary trend, but as a continuation of one of many branches of the multifaceted lineage of beings known as vertebrates. We exist as anatomically "modern" humans of the genus *Homo, which* has a fossil record that extends back a mere 2 million years. Of several species of *Homo* that once existed, *Homo sapiens* is the last. In one sense, we are the last of our kind. In another sense, humans represent one of the most remarkably oddball outcomes in the entire 500 million-year evolutionary history of the vertebrates, because what other creature is capable of contemplating, writing, and reading about its own existence?

Paleoanthropologist John Fleagle of the State University of New York at Stony Brook reminds us that **hominins** did not possess, from their very start, the familiar attributes that clearly distinguish humans from their ape relatives: **bipedal** locomotion, enlarged brains, grasping hands, and the use of tools and language. Hominins that date from the earliest known species such as *Sahelanthropus* (late Miocene, 6 million to 7 million years ago, Chad) and especially the well-documented *Australopithecus* (3.3 to 4.2 million years ago, southern and eastern Africa) did not emerge with all of these distinguishing anatomical and behavioral traits intact. In Fleagle's words, "The fossil record of *Australopithecus* provides direct evidence that the cluster of features characterizing living humans are not necessarily linked but rather evolved one by one." This chapter explores the emergence of the genus *Homo* by the end of the Pliocene Epoch as a species distinct from other early hominins.

FROM APES TO EARLY HOMININS

Another book in this series, *Primates and Human Ancestors*, details the evolutionary history that led to the apes and early humans. To summarize, the hub of ape evolution was in eastern Africa, in an area now known as the Great Rift Valley. During the Miocene Epoch, this area was the scene of frequent volcanic activity. Rift making and mountain building were widespread from Africa through Eurasia. The Arabian Peninsula was extended, the Tethys Sea shrank and broke up, and the climate grew increasingly arid. The effect on primate populations was significant as wide-open grasslands and savannas supplanted tropical forests. Apes of many kinds not only flourished during the late Miocene, but also adapted well to most of these environments.

The earliest fossils of true apes are known from eastern African regions of Kenya, Namibia, Uganda, and Ethiopia. As the ancestral lineages of apes diminished by the end of the Miocene, the lineages also split onto two evolutionary paths. One path diverged between 13 million and 15 million years ago and led to the genus *Pongo*—the orangutans. The other path led to modern African apes and eventually to humans, which split from the lineage of the genus *Pan* (chimpanzees) between 5 million and 7 million years ago.

Fossil clues to the existence of possible early hominins can be found in rocks that date from between 5 million and 7 million years ago, in the late Miocene Epoch. It is clear that by about 4.2 million years ago, in the Pliocene, ancestral humans were well established on the savannas of Africa. The telltale signs of early human species for which **paleontologists** search include anatomical evidence of bipedal locomotion; modified dental batteries with reduced canines and a thickening of tooth enamel on the molars; and skull morphology, among others. Behavioral traits, including the use of tools and the development of language, can also be found in ancestral humans prior to *Homo*. Examination of the fossil record quickly shows that

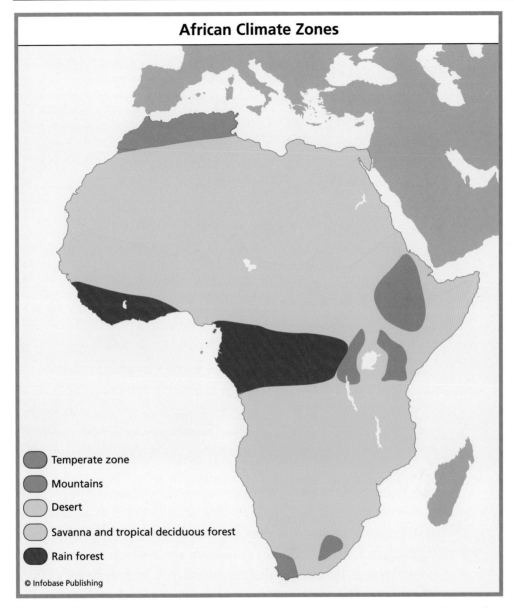

African Climate Zones

Temperate zone

Mountains

Desert

Savanna and tropical deciduous forest

Rain forest

© Infobase Publishing

Today's African climate zones were similar to those seen in Africa during the Miocene/
Pliocene Epochs.

these traits did not develop all at once, or even in a single species of
ancestral human, but occurred in stages over the course of several
hundred thousand years.

An artist's view of an Australopithecus afarensis scene

The best-represented hominin species prior to *Homo* include those of the genus *Australopithecus* ("southern ape"), which is known from several species that ranged widely in southern and eastern Africa from about 4.2 million to 1 million years ago. The cradle of human evolution is believed to be this region of Africa, with early humans gradually radiating out of Africa to other regions, including Asia and Europe.

Scientific descriptions of fragmentary specimens of early hominins go back to the mid-nineteenth century, but one of the first truly revealing early hominin specimens was found in South Africa in

1924 and described by Raymond Dart (1893–1988), an Australian anatomist. Discovered in a limestone quarry in the small town of Taung, the fossil consisted of a small skull that Dart painstakingly extracted from the tough rocky matrix in which it was sealed. The result was a lovely specimen of a juvenile skull. Dart had reason to believe that he was holding something more than the skull of an ape child. The specimen lacked the large canine teeth of apes, and its *foramen magnum*—the opening in the skull where the neck is connected to the spine—was positioned underneath the skull instead of at the **posterior**, indicating an upright posture. The specimen became popularly known as the "Taung child" because of its small size; Dart gave it the scientific name of *Australopithecus africanus* ("southern ape of Africa"). Dart described the specimen, which was between 2.4 million and 3 million years old, as a **transitional** stage between apes and humans. The genus *Australopithecus* is now considered a hominin and was the first of its kind to be described.

Following initial discoveries in South Africa, the search for early hominins broadened to East Africa. East Africa has produced many extraordinary hominin specimens from the geologically rugged area known as the Great Rift Valley. It is among the many specimens of *Australopithecus* from the Pliocene Epoch of southern and eastern Africa that the clearest picture of the biological evolution of early humans is evident. These hominins used their bipedal mode of walking to extend their geographic range and exploit new lands and food sources. The genus *Australopithecus* is perhaps the best candidate for a direct ancestor of *Homo*. **Australopithecines** existed for much of the Pliocene Epoch, and their apparent **extinction** coincides closely with the appearance of the first *Homo* species. Australopithecines were clearly bipedal, their molars had the distinctively thick enamel characteristic of early hominins, and there were measurable increases in the size of their brains during the 2 million years of their existence. The accompanying diagram depicts the various known lineages of early hominins of the Pliocene Epoch, leading to the rise of the species *Homo*.

Raymond Dart at a fossil site in South Africa. Dart discovered the small skull of the "Taung child" and realized that it showed the early stages of human evolution.

Comparison of Foramen Magnum

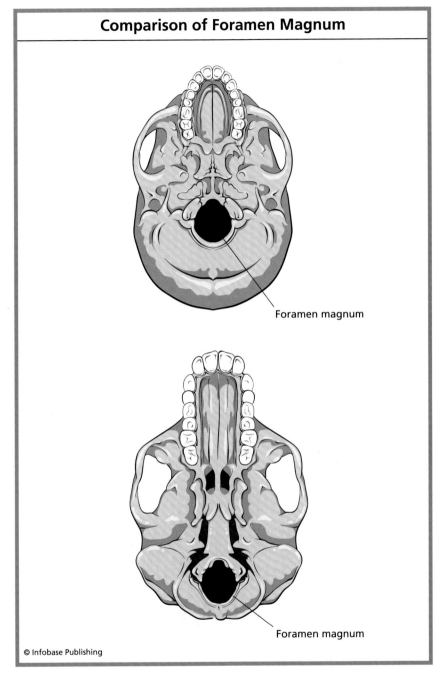

Foramen magnum

Foramen magnum

The position of the *foramen magnum* in modern humans (top) is placed further forward than in chimpanzees (bottom).

Timeline of Archaic Hominin Species

Million Years Ago

| 7 | 6 | 5 | 4 | 3 | 2 | 1 |

Early *Homo*

Australopithecus robustus

Australopithecus boisei

Australopithecus aethiopicus

Australopithecus garhi

Australopithecus africanus

Kenyanthropus platyops

Australopithecus afarensis

Australopithecus anamensis

Ardipithecus ramidus

Orrorin tugenensis

Sahelanthropus tchadensis

© Infobase Publishing

Timeline of archaic hominin species

WHAT IS A HOMININ?

Hominins are classified as part of the line of higher primates known as the Hominoidea. This line has three subgroups: the hylobatidae (gibbons and siamangs); the pongidae (pongo-orangutan); and the hominidae (African apes, including hominins). Current fossil and genetic evidence shows that apes arose about 20 million to 25 million years ago in Africa, Turkey, and eastern Europe and diversified into numerous lineages that spread throughout the **Old World**. The diagram "Primate Clades Leading to Hominins" depicts the general lineage of hominins within the primates.

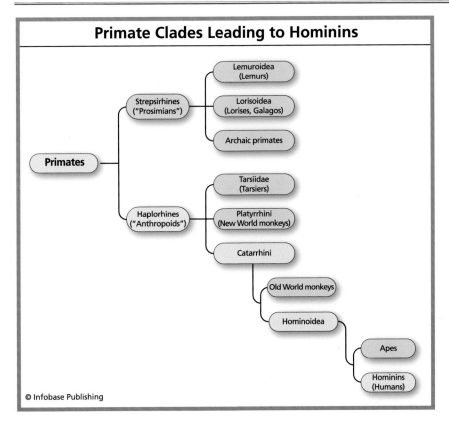

Primate Clades Leading to Hominins

© Infobase Publishing

This classification of hominins is based on biological and genetic evidence that classifies humans within the Hominidae, or hominoids. In defining hominins by their physical traits, the most direct description is that hominins are bipedal apes. Hominins have an extremely close genetic relationship with the African apes. Large brains, social living, a long gestation period and extended childhood all are characteristics found to some degree in nonhuman primates and in humans. Finding which of the apes are most closely related to humans required a comparison of human and chimpanzee **genomes**. The publication in 2005 of the chimpanzee genome by a research group known as the Chimpanzee Sequencing and Analysis

(continues on page 30)

THINK ABOUT IT

The Shady Discovery of a Missing Link

Charles Darwin's **theory** of evolution by **natural selection**, first published in 1859, ignited a firestorm of debate and scientific inquiry. In his own writings, Darwin speculated that if the fossil remains of an ancestral human were to be found, it probably would exhibit a combination of ape and human features—an especially big brain in an apelike skull, for example. Darwin's basis for thinking this way was the close association that he and others observed in the development of great apes and humans. Hence, the search for a so-called "missing link" was begun in scientific institutions and in the popular press of the time.

By the early twentieth century, not many fossils of possible early humans had yet been discovered. Of the few remains that had come to light in Europe and Asia, none came close to fulfilling the requirements of a "missing link." It is at this point that this scientific tale begins to go off course. Many reputable fossil hunters understood the importance of remaining objective in their fieldwork and letting their fossil finds speak for themselves. Others, however, were driven by a desire to find a "missing link" that would fit neatly into Darwin's puzzle and provide clear proof of the descent of humans from apes.

It was within this historical context that the announcement of Piltdown Man caused a great sensation in the year 1912. Revealed by amateur geologist Charles Dawson (1864–1916) at a meeting of the Geological Society of London, the original specimen consisted of several skull fragments and appeared to be remarkably old. Dawson claimed to have been given the pieces by workers at the Piltdown gravel yard in Sussex, England. Dawson gained the enthusiastic support of geologist Arthur Smith Woodward (1864–1944) of the British Museum, and the two returned to the roadside gravel site to look for more fossils. Remarkably, they found additional skull fragments and pieces of the lower jaw that appeared to be a part of the same specimen.

Enthusiasm for the "discovery" grew rapidly, and Dawson enlisted additional institutional support for his claim from British scientists Arthur

Keith (1866–1965) and Grafton Elliot Smith (1871–1937). Dawson named the specimen *Eoanthropus dawsonoi* ("Dawson's dawn man") after himself—a display of bad manners in scientific circles that should have set off alarm bells far and wide. What Dawson and his colleagues had announced was nothing less than the perfectly conceived skull of a "missing link," a large brained, apelike creature that was half human and half ape.

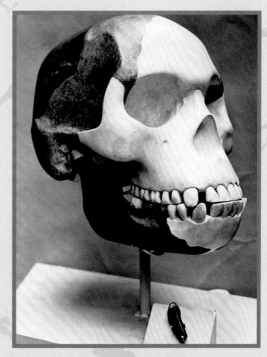

Piltdown Man—A hoax specimen

Popularly known as the Piltdown Man, the discovery was eagerly accepted by British scientists but did attract the criticism of scientists from foreign shores. Amazingly, every time the heat was on, Dawson just happened to discover another important piece of the skull. Dawson died in 1916, but his legacy lived on for many years. Some important fossil discoveries that followed soon thereafter, including the discovery of *Australopithecus africanus* in southern Africa in 1924, were largely ignored at the time because they did not meet the requirements already fulfilled by Piltdown Man: those of a large-brained, ancestral apelike creature.

(continues)

(continued)

Gradually, an accumulating body of counterevidence for the nature of early hominins led to a closer examination of Piltdown Man. In 1953, using newly devised fluorine dating methods, scientists proved conclusively that the skull and jaw of Piltdown Man were not prehistoric but of relatively recent origin. The skull was human and about 600 years old, and the lower jaw was from a recently deceased orangutan. All of the fragments had been carefully discolored with chemicals and distressed to give the appearance of having come from the same time. Piltdown Man was a fake.

By the time Piltdown Man was proved to be a ruse, most of the perpetrators were long gone. The mystery of who was behind the forgery continued until only recently. Two pieces of the puzzle have now come to light. A storage trunk containing similarly dyed and distressed fake fossil bones—presumably tests for the Piltdown hoax—were found in the attic of the Natural History Museum of London. The trunk belonged to Martin Hinton, a curator of zoology at the museum at the time of the hoax. Analysis showed that the chemicals used to discolor the bones in Hinton's trunk were identical to the chemicals used to discolor the Piltdown "specimen."

It appears that the forger has been found, but what was his motive? Research by Professor Brian Gardiner of King's College, London, suggests that Hinton had a grudge against his superior at the museum, Charles Dawson's possibly unwitting collaborator Arthur Smith Woodward. Additional research in 2003 by British archaeologist Miles Russell proved Hinton had the means to implicate his boss. It turns out that Charles Dawson

(continued from page 27)

Consortium revealed that the genetic makeup of humans is only 2.7 percent different from that of chimps, making them our closest relatives among the great apes.

The study of evolutionary genetics sometimes affects the way that organisms are classified. Recent molecular studies of **anthropoid**

Hinton and Dawson at the scene of the hoax

had a history of creating antique and scientific forgeries even prior to his "discovery" of Piltdown Man. Dawson and Hinton apparently conspired to create the Piltdown hoax, Dawson for the fame it would bring, and Hinton for the secret pleasure of besmirching the reputation of his superior.

genetic evolution have led to a change in the terminology used to describe humans and their most immediate ancestors. Previously, the term *hominid* was used to describe all gorillas, chimpanzees, and humans. Recent **gene** studies have revealed, however, that orangutans split from the great ape line earlier than was once thought. This means that humans, gorillas, and chimpanzees are more closely related to one another than any of them are to orangutans. For the purpose of classification, the hominoids were divided into two subgroups, the Pongidae (orangutans) and the Homininae (gorillas, chimpanzees, and humans and their ancestors). Furthermore, the term *hominin* is reserved exclusively for humans and ancestral humans since the time of their divergence from the other great apes. Therefore, humans and their ancestors are now referred to as *hominins* instead of *hominids*.

EVOLUTIONARY TRENDS LEADING TO *HOMO*

The anatomical and behavioral traits that distinguish hominins from the great apes did not appear suddenly with a bang. The traits developed quietly, over the course of more than 4 million years. The heights of human development represented by the appearance of language, religious beliefs, and art are relatively recent phenomena in hominin history: None occurred earlier than 200,000 years ago, and most occurred much more recently than that. Such late-appearing behavioral characteristics of humans were made possible by a foundation of more slowly evolving anatomical traits, traces of which can be seen in specimens of ancestral humans.

The key anatomical traits associated with hominin evolution include bipedal locomotion; reduction of the canine teeth; reduction in the size of the molar teeth and an associated increase in the thickness of the molar tooth enamel; and an enlarged brain. Tooth enamel was thicker in earlier hominin species than in *Homo*. The dramatic enlargement of the brain was a characteristic of *Homo* rather than australopithecines. Fossils of early hominins tell a variety of stories regarding the appearance and timing of these **derived** traits. These stories strongly suggest that the evolution of hominins did not occur as a straight line of connected lineage but perhaps as several independently developing species in which the occurrence of these traits coevolved at different times.

The earliest possible hominin specimens include a trio of species that date from just before the beginning of the Pliocene Epoch. They are known from fragmentary evidence, and their position as hominins is a matter of much debate among paleoanthropologists.

Yet, these specimens include some homininlike features that represent either evidence of ancestral human species or a transitional phase in the development of great apes with some homininlike features.

Early Hominins

Sahelanthropus tchadensis (late Miocene, 6 million to 7 million years ago, Chad)

Discovered in north-central Africa in 2001, *Sahelanthropus tchadensis* consists of a nearly complete cranium, a mandible (lower jaw) and several isolated teeth. The specimen is dated to about 7 million years ago. Reconstruction of the skull suggests that the *foramen magnum* was positioned far enough beneath the skull to accommodate a bipedal posture. This claim has been debated actively by many, including paleoanthropologist Milford H. Wolpoff, who believes that *Sahelanthropus* probably was an ape showing some transitional features of the skull and jaw. Wolpoff disputes the interpretation of the *foramen magnum* because of the incompleteness of the material; he argues that the **anatomy** of the face and jaws clearly shows that *Sahelanthropus* did not normally hold its head upright. Furthermore, the braincase was small—about 350 cubic centimeters (cc)—about the size of that of a chimpanzee and smaller than those of early hominins from the Pliocene Epoch.

Orrorin tugenensis (late Miocene, 6 million years ago, Kenya)

Discovered in Kenya in 2000, *Orrorin tugenensis* is known from dental and **postcranial** skeletal elements from deposits that date from 6 million years ago. The fragmentary remains make it difficult to ascertain with certainty whether *Orrorin tugenensis* was a hominin or an ape. Parts of a thigh bone provide some **diagnostic traits**, but this material is not enough by itself to indicate bipedalism with certainty. The front teeth of *Orrorin tugenensis* were more apelike, but the molars had a more square shape like those of hominins. The long, apelike canines argue against *Orrorin tugenensis* being a hominin, however.

Ardipithecus kadabba and *Ardipithecus ramidus* (early Pliocene to late Miocene, 4.4 million to 5.8 million years ago, Ethiopia)

These specimens were discovered in 1992 in northern Ethiopia, where digs have yielded fragmentary remains of more than two dozen homininlike individuals. These originally were thought to be fossils of *Australopithecus*, but differences in the tooth enamel, the limb structure, and the position of the *foramen magnum* suggest that these species were less derived and warranted their own genus designation.

The name *Ardipithecus ramidus* ("ground-living root hominin") was given to the first specimens. Additional specimens were announced in 2004 that were even older: They dated from as long ago as 5.8 million years. These older specimens were even more apelike and were assigned their own separate species, *Ardipithecus kadabba*. Genus *Ardipithecus* had several traits that link it more closely to apes—these include thin tooth enamel and large canine teeth. The most homininlike characteristic of *Ardipithecus* was represented by the more forward position of the *foramen magnum* at the base of the skull. Although it is not as far forward as in *Homo*, the *foramen magnum* in *Ardipithecus* is positioned farther forward than in a quadrupedal ape such as a chimpanzee. One interpretation of this specimen is that it was at the base of the hominin divergence from the great apes and displayed a more upright, though possibly not fully erect, bipedal posture.

The anatomy of the earliest possible hominins such *Sahelanthropus, Orrorin* and *Ardipithecus* shows that changes were developing in these creatures that were echoed more fully in later hominins, beginning with *Australopithecus*. The presence of bipedalism in one or more of these specimens suggests that the ability to walk on two legs was one of the first **adaptations** leading to the more derived hominins. The presence of large canine teeth, weak molar enamel, and small brains suggests that these early hominin wannabes were still anchored in the lineage of the great apes. Of these three specimens, *Ardipithecus* remains the best candidate for being a part of the hominin lineage, whether as a directly ancestor to *Australopithecus* or as a sister taxon that split off and evolved independently.

The Genus *Australopithecus*: The Best Understood Early Hominins

Even the best of the early hominin species from the late Miocene lack a complete suite of the anatomical traits that are normally associated with hominins. Most of these species were clearly apelike, with only hints of such homininlike features as bipedalism and a modification of the dental battery away from shearing to chewing and grinding. The picture of early hominins becomes much clearer in the more recent fossil remains from the Pliocene Epoch of eastern and southern Africa. Represented most significantly by dozens of specimens of the genus *Australopithecus*, these remains provide the best clues to the roots of *Homo* ancestry.

The genus *Australopithecus* first appears in the fossil record about 4.2 million years ago. *Australopithecus* represents the first ancestral human genus that contains—to one degree or another— all of the hallmark anatomical traits associated with hominins. *Australopithecus* is the best candidate for a direct ancestor of *Homo,* and it is probably from one species of *Australopithecus* that the lineage of modern humans arose. The exact relationship between these ancestral species and modern humans remains a hotly debated topic, however, as is discussed in Chapter 2.

There are several recognized species of *Australopithecus* as well as some lesser-known taxa whose affinity will remain uncertain until additional fossil evidence is found. The most widely known and accepted taxa include *A. anamensis, A. afarensis,* and *A. africanus* from the middle to late Pliocene. These taxa are the most likely candidates for having an ancestral relationship with the genus *Homo.*

Another well-known group of australopithecines dates from the later Pliocene (1.3 million to 2.6 million years ago). Members of this group sometimes are referred to as **robust** species because of their relatively larger body size; their large cheek teeth; their wide cheekbones; and their low, sloping foreheads with a crested ridge down the centerline of the skull for the attachment of powerful jaw muscles. The robust australopithecines are widely accepted as having split off from the line of australopithecines that led to the rise of modern humans. Some robust species probably coexisted with early *Homo* but were extinct by the Early Pleistocene Epoch, about 1.3 million years ago. For these reasons, robust australopithecines are not included in the discussion that follows about the ancestry of modern humans.

When looking for evolutionary links between *Homo* and *Australopithecus,* one sees that a number of derived anatomical traits are apparent in the fossil evidence of these early hominins. The evolutionary links between different *Australopithecus* taxa are much debated. Nevertheless, there is a general trend in australopithecines toward increasingly derived features that occur over the course of about 700,000 years in the evolution of this genus.

Anatomical Trends of Australopithecines

Bipedalism and Locomotion. Early australopithecines, including *A. afarensis* and *A. africanus*, were clearly bipedal but also may have been partly tree climbing because of their long arms and, in the case of *A. afarensis*, curved fingers. *A. afarensis* is known from more than 70 specimens, making it the best-understood species of ancestral human. Discovered and first described in 1974 by American paleontologist Donald Johanson, the first specimen was that of a small female that measured only 3.5 feet (1 m) tall. It was nicknamed "Lucy." In addition to Lucy, additional specimens of this genus have been found that represent adult individuals.

With as much as 60 percent of its postcranial skeleton represented by a composite of fossil specimens, *A. afarensis* provides a clear picture of the posture of this species. The *foramen magnum* was located more forward than that of a chimpanzee but not quite as forward as that of *Homo*. This would have given Lucy a clearly bipedal posture but with a slight stoop. *A. afaensis* had arms that were relatively long and legs that were short in comparison to *Homo*, but Wolpoff points out that it is important to compare Lucy's limbs with those of chimpanzees to best understand the evolutionary trend represented by *A. afarensis*. Lucy's arms, although long enough to enable skilled tree climbing, were proportionally shorter than those of a chimpanzee. The change in arm length in Lucy marked a trend toward shorter arms and longer legs that is seen in later hominins.

Head Postures

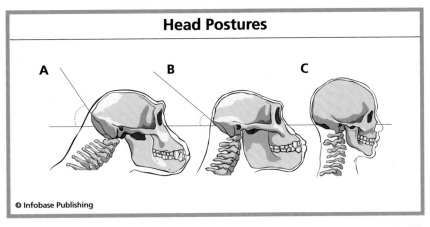

© Infobase Publishing

The progressively upright head posture of chimpanzees (A), *A. afarensis* (B) and *H. sapiens* (C).

A. africanus had a body plan similar to that of *A. afarensis*, with a few exceptions. *A. africanus* also was a natural biped, but its arms were shorter. Its body was more funnel shaped than that of either Lucy or *Homo*.

Dentition. The trend in dentition from apes to hominins involves several aspects of tooth, jaw, and skull design. Ape jaws generally have larger front teeth and very large canines. The canines work together with large, sharp-edged premolars with single cusps to shear off food, almost in the manner of a pair of scissors. The molars of apes are small and not heavily enameled; this makes them less generalized for grinding a wide variety of foods. The dental battery in apes is long and U-shaped, and there is a noticeable gap between the front teeth (the incisors) and the canines. This gap provides room for the canines when the jaw is closed. The massiveness of the jaw and the front teeth in some apes results in a jutting forward of the jaw called **prognathism**. In some apes, the jaw muscles are massive and required the development of a **sagittal crest** along the top of the skull to accommodate muscle attachment.

In contrast to that of apes, the human dental battery has smaller front teeth and greatly reduced canines that have lost the shearing action found in apes. There is no gap between the front teeth and the canines, and the premolar is a smaller, nonshearing tooth with two

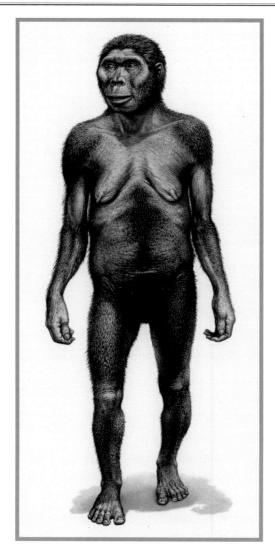

Australopithecus afarensis—"Lucy"

cusps. Molars in archaic humans are very large, heavily enameled, and adapted for the grinding of many kinds of foods; they become reduced in size and less heavily enameled in modern humans. The overall dental battery is parabolic rather than U-shaped. A reduction, in humans, in the size of the jaw and the front teeth resulted in a jaw that jutted out somewhat less than in apes.

These trends in dentition and skull design are seen in various stages in the evolution of australopithecines. *A. anamensis* and *A. afarensis* were generally more apelike in their dentition, with large canines, large premolars, and a U-shaped tooth battery. The premolars of *A. afarensis* were single-cusped like those of a chimpanzee but intermediate in size between those of apes and *Homo*. The molars in each of these australopithecine taxa were enlarged, however, and showed thicker enamel. *A. africanus* was further along in the trend toward smaller, more generalized teeth with its reduced front incisors and canines, its smaller premolars, and its large, squared molars. The gap between the incisors and canines is also reduced in *A. africanus*, although the U-shape of the jaw is still intact. *A. africanus* also represented a trend toward a larger braincase.

Brain Size. The rapid evolution of the size of the hominin brain is certainly the most remarkable aspect of human evolution. As the

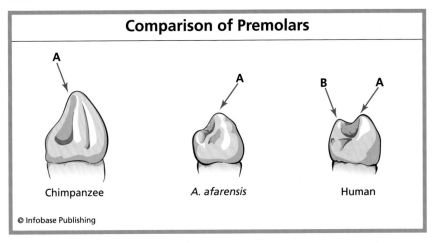

Comparison of Premolars

Chimpanzee

A. afarensis

Human

© Infobase Publishing

Human premolars have a primary cusp (a) and a secondary cusp (b), and have lost the shearing quality found in chimpanzees and *A. afarensis*.

hominin brain evolved, it grew bigger, and its **neural** connections reorganized to handle more complex processing functions. While modern technology such as magnetic resonance imaging (MRI) can aid today's scientists who study the way the brain works in living individuals, paleontologists must turn to fossil evidence to ascertain how and when the hominin brain changed in ancestral humans. Even though the brain itself is never fossilized, its size, shape, and neural connections can be determined by making an **endocast** of the brain-case. An endocast is a cast made of the brain cavity inside the skull. Along with the general shape and organization of the brain, an endo-cast reveals the impressions made on the skull walls by the outside surface of the brain. This information can reveal much about the size, shape, organization, and capacity of the brains of extinct creatures.

The fossil record of australopithecines shows that their cranial capacity remained almost the same—from about 400 to 530 cubic centimeters—for 2 million years. Then, with the coming of various *Homo* species, brain capacity expanded dramatically, from about 630 cc 2 million years ago to some 1,400 cc by about 300,000 years ago. The brain capacity of hominins has increased by about 400 percent over the past 3.5 million years. Among the australopithecines being discussed,

A. africanus showed a marked increase in the size of the brain cavity over Lucy—550 cc compared with 450 cc—a trend one would expect in one of the youngest taxa of ancestral humans prior to *Homo.*

The table that follows compares the average cranial capacities and **encephalization quotients** (EQs) of fossil hominins. Also known as a brain-to-body-mass ratio, the EQ is a ratio that compares the actual brain mass of an animal with the expected brain mass of an animal of that size. The ratio becomes less meaningful when the body mass of an animal is exceptionally large and there are few comparisons to be made with other animals of the same size (e.g., the elephant, the blue whale). Devising a quotient such as the EQ provided an objective, measurable way to compare the potential for intelligence in an animal even when working with only an endocast of a fossil skull.

Sexual dimorphism. A species is said to be sexually dimorphic if there are marked differences in the physical size and shape of anatomical features between males and females. In living animals, **sexual dimorphism** also encompasses color, as in the color of bird feathers, reptile skin, and mammal hair. Because fossils provide no clues to the outward appearance or color of a specimen,

AVERAGE CRANIAL CAPACITIES FOR FOSSIL HOMINIDS (ADULT SPECIMENS ONLY)

Taxon	Number of Specimens	Average Cranial Capacity (CC)	Range (CC)	Estimated EQ
A. afarensis	2	450	400–500	1.87
A. africanus	7	445	405–500	2.16
A. robustus and A. boisei	7	507	475–530	2.50
H. habilis	7	631	509–775	2.73–3.38
H. erectus	22	1,003	650–1,251	3.27
Archaic *H. sapiens*	18	1,330	1,100–1,586	3.52
H. neanderthalensis	19	1,445	1,200–1,750	4.04
Modern *H. sapiens* (older than 8,000 years)	11	1,490	1,290–1,600	5.27

Sources: Aiello and Dean (1990), Kappelman (1996), and Holloway (1999).
Note: Estimated EQs are not derived using all the specimens included in the second column.

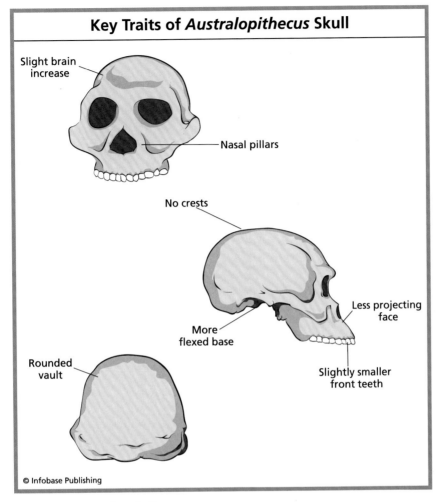

Key Traits of *Australopithecus* Skull

Slight brain increase

Nasal pillars

No crests

Less projecting face

More flexed base

Slightly smaller front teeth

Rounded vault

© Infobase Publishing

An australopithecine skull

however, paleoanthropologists look for anatomical differences between specimens that might be attributed to gender differences. In the great apes, sexual dimorphism generally is exhibited as differences in body size between males and females. Male apes normally have larger bodies than females. The canine teeth often are proportionately larger in males than in females as well. These same trends appear to occur in australopithecines. In *A. africanus*, female incisors remain proportionately the same size as those in males, but female canines and cheek teeth are reduced in size.

AUSTRALOPITHECUS TRAITS BY SPECIES*

Species	Earliest Date (mya)	Average Cranial Capacity (cc)	Estimated Body Weight (lbs/kg)	Locomotion	Dentition
Australopithecus anamensis	4.2	unknown	95/43	Bipedal and possibly arboreal	More apelike: large canines; large premolars; large molars with thick enamel
Australopithecus afarensis	3.9	450	99/44.7	Bipedal and arboreal	More apelike: somewhat smaller canines and premolars; parallel tooth rows; large molars with thick enamel
Australopithecus africanus	3.5	450–550	91/41.3	Mostly bipedal, but somewhat arboreal	More humanlike: small front teeth, including canines; small premolars and molars

*males
Based on Wolpoff (1999), Stanford (2006), and Fuentes (2007)

An exhaustive study of the *A. afarensis* fossil record was published in 2003 by anthropologist Philip Reno of Kent State University and others. This study concluded that the Lucy genus expressed the same kinds and proportions of physical differences between the sexes as modern humans. A 2004 study by anthropologist S.-H. Lee of the University of California, Riverside, used different statistical methods and came to a somewhat different conclusion, however. The 2004 study found that "*A. afarensis* is similar in size sexual dimorphism to gorillas in femoral [upper leg bone] variables, to humans in humeral [upper arm bone] variables, and to chimpanzees in canine variables." The studies showed that the pattern of sexual dimorphism found in *A. afarensis* is a unique mosaic of patterns seen in living apes and humans. The differences between these two studies probably are due to the small sample size for some of the bones being compared. Looking at the three humeral bones available for *A. afarensis*, it is not really certain which might be from a male and which from a female, so each study (as well as those by earlier researchers) based its assessment on some other **morphological** character of the arm bones that may or may not be due to sexual dimorphism. Even though their results disagree somewhat, each of these studies shows a trend in hominin evolution toward less extreme size differences in many physical features of male and female hominins when compared with some great apes such as gorillas.

APPROACHING THE PLIOCENE-PLEISTOCENE BORDER

This fossil record of Pliocene hominins shows that australopithecines emerged from southern and eastern Africa in a variety of forms. Their evolution coincided with change in the African habitat that created a more arid world that consisted of forested areas and grassy plains. Australopithecines developed adaptations that enabled them to prosper during such changing times. These adaptations included bipedal locomotion and modifications to their teeth to make these hominins capable of adapting to a wide variety of foods, from the toughest nuts and seeds to soft vegetation. The robust australopithecines became highly specialized eaters, with powerful jaws and flat teeth for grinding tough, fibrous roots. This highly derived adaptation may have made it difficult for the robust australopithecines to adapt to other food sources.

Although they varied widely in the shape of the skull and dentition, australopithecines in general did not show an evolutionary trend toward increased body size or cranial capacity. Most were small creatures, standing around 5 feet (1.5 m) tall and weighing between 90 and 100 pounds (41 and 45 kg). Two taxa of australopithecines, *A. afarensis* and *A. africanus*, had less robust skulls and a general reduction in the size of their dentition. *A. africanus* in particular showed a trend toward larger brain size. It is probably from these ancestral lines that the first *Homo* species arose around the time of the Pliocene-Pleistocene border.

Chapter 2 will explore the rapid rise, diversification, and radiation of the first species of *Homo*.

SUMMARY

This chapter explored the emergence, by the end of the Pliocene Epoch, of the genus *Homo* as a species distinct from other early hominins.

1. Hominin traits—including bipedalism, modified dentition, and increased brain size—did not appear at once in ancestral humans. These traits appeared gradually over time in different lineages of early hominins.

2. The best-represented hominin species prior to *Homo* include those of the genus *Australopithecus* ("southern ape"). This genus is known from several species that ranged widely in southern and eastern Africa from about 4.2 million to 1 million years ago.

3. The cradle of human evolution is believed to be East Africa. Early humans gradually radiated out of Africa to other regions, including Asia and Europe.

4. Hominins are classified as part of the line of higher primates known as the Hominoidea. This line includes three subgroups: the hylobatidae (gibbons and siamangs), the pongidae (pongo-orangutan), and the hominidae (African apes, including hominins).

5. Hominins have an extremely close genetic relationship with the great apes. The genetic makeup of humans is only 2.7% different from that of chimps. This makes chimpanzees our closest relatives among the great apes.

6. The key anatomical traits associated with hominin evolution include bipedal locomotion, reduction of the canine teeth, reduction in the size of the molar teeth and associated increase in the thickness of the molar tooth enamel, and an enlarged brain.

7. The most widely known and accepted taxa of *Australopithecus* are *A. anamensis*, *A. afarensis*, and *A. africanus*, from the middle to late Pliocene of southern and eastern Africa. These taxa are the most likely candidates for having an ancestral relationship with the genus *Homo*.

8. The robust australopithecines probably split off from the line of australopithecines that led to the rise of modern humans.

9. The fossil record of australopithecines shows that their cranial capacity remained almost the same—from about 400 to 530 cc for two million years.

10. Studies of sexual dimorphism in *A. afarensis* show a trend in hominin evolution toward less extreme size differences in many physical features of male and female hominins when compared with some great apes such as gorillas.

ARCHAIC *HOMO* SPECIES

Between the demise of the last species of *Australopithecus*, some 1.2 million years ago, and the establishment of modern humans of the species *Homo sapiens*, about 200,000 years ago, there is a gulf in time that is filled with many intriguing clues to the evolution of modern humans. During that span, the taxon *Homo* not only arose, but also rapidly eclipsed its ancestors in several astonishing ways. *Homo* species developed into the tallest hominins, adapted a dental battery of smaller teeth capable of eating a diversity of food types, and evolved brains that today are roughly three times larger than those of the most advanced australopithecines.

In piecing together the fossil history of *Homo*, there is considerable debate among paleoanthropologists as to when the **speciation** of *Homo* began. There is also considerable debate as to which specimens prior to 1.5 million years ago should be assigned to the genus *Homo* and which to *Australopithecus*. The disagreement is partly due to a lack of informative specimens but is also due to disagreements about how to define *Homo* as a genus.

This chapter traces the discoveries of early *Homo*, describes key specimens, and discusses problems of establishing evolutionary links between modern *Homo* and ancestral humans.

DEFINING EARLY *HOMO* SPECIES

Understanding which fossil hominins represent the first species of *Homo* is a controversial matter. All hominins were bipedal, had larger brains than their great ape ancestors, and developed a parabolic dental battery, yet there are many differences between species of early hominins in all of these regards. Generally speaking, early hominins become candidates for the genus *Homo* when their anatomical features resemble those seen in modern humans more closely than they resemble those seen in australopithecines.

If *Australopithecus* represents the last hominin species prior to *Homo*, then every hominin species that existed between the decline of *Australopithecus* and the rise of *Homo sapiens*—a span of about 1.8 million years—can be examined on a sliding scale of features leading to modern humans. Because evolution is such a gradual process, there are several stages of development leading to modern *Homo*. While there is much less controversy over the appearance of *Homo sapiens* about 200,000 years ago, much disagreement still exists regarding the interpretation of fossils representing earlier *Homo* species. This is due to a lack of complete fossil evidence—a problem that scientists hope will be reduced over time with the discovery of still more early specimens.

The accompanying table represents some of the features that paleoanthropologists consider in assigning hominin specimens to species of *Australopithecus* or *Homo*. Note that in addition to skeletal remains, the presence of tools at early hominin sites is considered to be a calling card left by a *Homo* species—clear evidence of the increased intelligence and problem-solving and planning skills that marked an advance over australopithecines. There is, however, some evidence that at least one line of australopithecines—*A. garhi* (2.5 million to 2.6 million years ago, Ethiopia)—may have developed primitive stone tools similar to the Olduwan tools associated with *Homo habilis*.

The earliest discoveries of *Homo* species of great significance were found in Asia. These included such historic finds as Java Man and Peking Man (or *Beijing Man*, based on the modern spelling of the capital city of China). Java Man was discovered in 1891 in East Java, Indonesia, by Dutch anatomist and fossil hunter Eugène Dubois (1858–1940). Dubois's decision to search for specimens of early humans in Indonesia went against the conventional wisdom of the time, which assumed an African origin for the human species. Dubois, however, was intrigued by the vast network of undisturbed

TRENDS IN HOMININ EVOLUTION

Features	*Australopithecus* Traits	*Homo* Traits
Skull and cranea	Smaller brain Larger face in proportion to overall skull Face often flat or concave Large to moderate brow Sagittal crest (some) Protruding jaw Receding chin Thinner braincase wall	Larger brain Smaller face in proportion to overall skull Face never concave Large to slight brow Vertical forehead Domed cranium, no sagittal crest Chin may protrude Thicker braincase wall
Teeth	U-shaped dental battery Massive jaw Larger incisors and canines Very large premolars and molars, heavily enameled	Parabolic-shaped dental battery Less massive jaw Small incisors and canines Smaller premolars and molars, not heavily enameled
Limbs	Longer arms Shorter legs Curved fingers (climbing) Limited grasping capability in hands Heavier (thicker) postcranial bones	Shorter arms Longer legs, greater height Grasping fingers, thumb, precision grip Lighter (thinner) postcranial bones
Torso	Funnel shaped Mostly upright	Cylindrically shaped Fully upright
Tools	Possible early stone tools	Early stone toolmaking

caves in Java; and he reasoned that fossils might be found in them, just as they often were in Europe.

Dubois's gamble paid off, after several difficult years of field-work, with a small assemblage of hominin bones to which he gave the scientific name *Pithecanthropus erectus*—"upright ape man." The specimen, possibly a composite of several individuals, was fragmentary, but it provided tantalizing clues to a possible transitional stage of evolution between the great apes and humans. It became known as Java Man and was widely touted, even by Dubois, as the "missing link" between modern humans and apes. The specimen consisted of a skull cap, the cranial capacity of which was larger than that of apes; a leg bone that showed characteristics of upright posture; and a few teeth. The specimen was dated to approximately

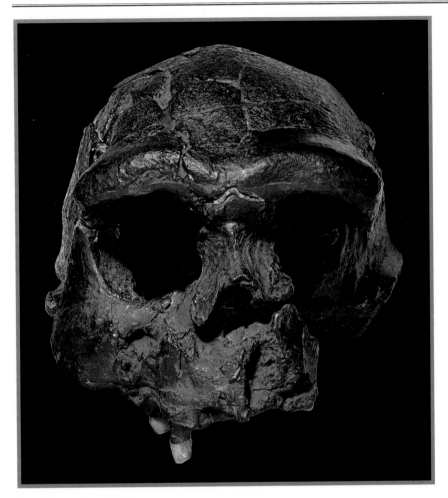

Java Man—*H. erectus*

700,000 years ago and was at that time the oldest known specimen of a hominin.

The remains of Peking Man were first discovered near the capital of China during the middle 1920s by several expeditions of Western and Chinese paleontologists. Expeditions led by Swedish geologist Johan Gunnar Andersson (1874–1960) and American paleontologist Walter W. Granger (1872–1941) were the first to uncover evidence of hominins at the fossil site, between 1921 and 1926. The specimens consisted only of teeth, however. A Canadian

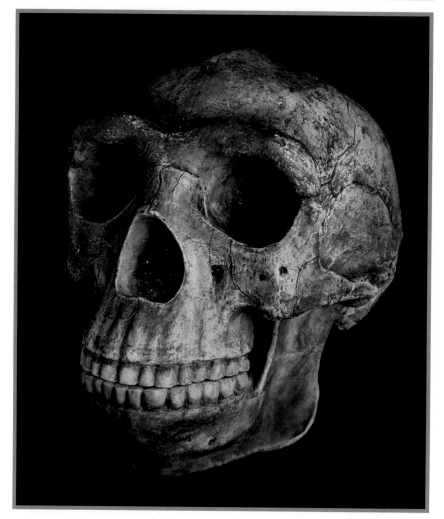

Peking Man—*H. erectus*

anatomist who lived in China, Davidson Black (1884–1934) of Peking Union Medical College, resumed excavations in 1927 and found additional teeth. Black published a scientific description of the specimen and gave it the species name *Sinanthropus pekinensis* ("Chinese primal man of Peking"), although many paleoanthropologists criticized the naming of a new species based solely on fossil teeth.

Black was soon vindicated. Continued excavations at the Chinese site between 1929 and 1937 yielded at least 14 partial craniums, 11 lower jaws, additional teeth, postcranial skeleton elements, and even stone tools. Peking Man has been dated to about 500,000 years ago. Both Java Man and Peking Man are now referred to the species *Homo erectus*, a more ancient lineage than *H. sapiens* with roots in Africa.

The discoveries of Java Man and Peking Man temporarily turned the search for the first humans toward Asia. By the 1930s, however, after the work of Louis Leakey (1903–1972) and others in East Africa, it became clear that the remains of humans that were being found in Asia were merely evidence of an earlier radiation of hominins out of Africa.

The earliest known *Homo* species is that of *Homo habilis*, the "handy man," named by Louis Leakey and his colleagues in 1964. The original *H. habilis* specimen was found in the Olduvai Gorge of Tanzania by Leakey and his wife, Mary Leakey (1913–1996). Because species of *Australopithecus* had been found in the same general location as this specimen, the discovery of *H. habilis* revealed, for the first time, that the two species lived and thrived together as contemporaries. Primitive stone tools had been found previously at Olduvai, but none of the hominins found previously in the area were likely candidates for having made such tools—the hominins found earlier had less dexterous hand anatomy and smaller brains. With the discovery of *H. habilis*, the Leakeys had also discovered the most likely makers of such tools.

The partial skull that figured most importantly in the Leakeys' discovery was significantly larger than that of *Australopithecus*. The cranial capacity of *H. habilis* was between 500 cc and 700 cc, whereas the cranial capacity of the East African *A. robustus* topped out at around 500 cc.

When the designation was first proposed in 1964, there was a reluctance to accept *H. habilis* as an early species of *Homo*. This was due in part to the fragmentary nature of the fossil evidence. It also was because the species appeared to have lived at the same

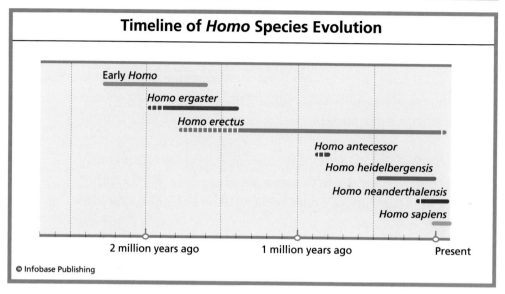

Timeline of *Homo* species evolution

time as the more primitive australopithecines found in the same area. This made it possible that *H. habilis* and the australopithecines were actually the same species showing a wider range of variation in cranial capacity than originally was thought. Additional discoveries since the initial description of *H. habilis* have confirmed the Leakeys' original diagnosis, however. This species of early *Homo* now is known from several craniums, limb bones, teeth, and other elements. *H. habilis* fossils range in age from about 1.6 million to 2.2 million years old.

There remains much debate about the ancestry of *Homo sapiens* and about the evolutionary relationship of *Homo sapiens* to earlier species of *Homo*. The accompanying chart provides a glimpse at the key species of early *Homo* that are currently recognized and shows their relationship in time only. This chart does not attempt to draw links between lineages of *Homo*, a discussion of which is found later in this chapter, in the section "A **Phylogeny** of Early *Homo*."

The following descriptions of ancestral *Homo* species recognize the species for which there is most consensus among scientists. Other

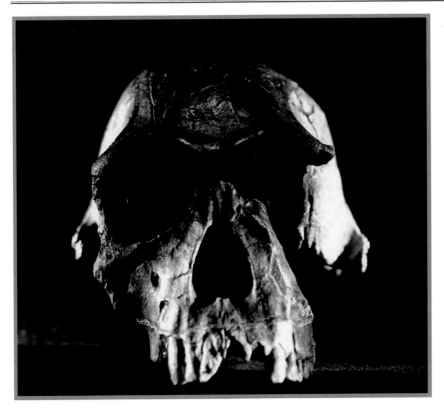

Skull of *H. habilis* found in Koobi Fora, Kenya

possible species are recognized by some. The earliest *Homo* species described here is *H. habilis,* but some paleoanthropologists split this species into more than one, usually *H. habilis* and *H. rudolfensis.* Similarly, *H. ergaster* and *H. erectus,* described here as two separate species, sometimes are combined into the single taxon of *H. erectus.*

Early Homo Species

Homo habilis (1.6 million to 2.2 million years ago, East Africa). Currently viewed as the earliest species of *Homo, H. habilis* was short compared with modern humans and retained the longer arms associated with its probable australopithecine ancestors. Specimens assigned to this taxon show much variation, leading to debate as to whether this material comprises one or more species. All of the specimens share some generalized traits such as having a smaller face, moderate to small brows, and a somewhat jutting jaw.

Specimens from the Olduvai Gorge area are smaller; they stand about 4 feet, 3 inches (1.3 m) tall and have a brain capacity that ranges from 503 to 661 cc. Specimens found in Koobi Fora, Kenya differ in a number of ways from those from the Olduvai Gorge in Tanzania. Known mostly from skull specimens, these Koobi Fora *Homo* specimens were larger individuals, perhaps standing 5 feet (1.5 m) tall. The Kenyan specimens are represented by two varieties. One variety had a smaller face, small back teeth, a moderate brow ridge, and a cranial capacity of about 510 cc. The other had a broader, flatter face but small brows, large back teeth, and a cranial capacity of 775 cc. The differences among these specimens from Olduvai and Koobi Fora suggest that these specimens actually might represent two or even three species. The name *Homo rudolfensis* is assigned by some scientists to the Kenyan specimens of *H. habilis*.

Homo ergaster (1.55 million to 1.78 million years ago, Kenya). *H. ergaster* ("working man") is another source of debate among paleoanthropologists. Specimens assigned to this taxon once were considered members of *Homo erectus*, one of the best-known species of early humans that is found primarily in Africa, Europe, and Asia. To some scientists, *H. ergaster* represents a subspecies of *H. erectus* rather than a line that developed separately. Like *H. erectus*, *H. ergaster* represented a significant increase in size for *Homo* over its predecessors. Standing up to 6 feet, 2 inches (1.8 m) tall, *H. ergaster* had an estimated cranial capacity of 750 to 800 cc, twice as large as that seen in australopithecines.

Notable differences between *H. ergaster* and *H. erectus* include thinner bones in the cranium of *H. ergaster*. A nearly complete juvenile specimen of *H. ergaster* known as the Turkana Boy was discovered in 1984 in Kenya. The shape of the pelvis and the number of erupted teeth suggested that the specimen represented a 12-year-old boy. This remarkably modern skeleton provides an excellent contrast to the other well-known juvenile early hominin skeleton, that of

H. erectus

Lucy, *Australopithecus afarensis*, a hominin that lived some 1 million years prior to *H. ergaster*. The two specimens provide a remarkable benchmark comparison of the evolution of derived traits from the time of ancestral hominins to the emergence of *Homo*.

Homo erectus (1.0 million to 1.8 million years ago, eastern and northern Africa, Europe, central Asia, Asia). *H. erectus* ("upright man") is widely known, both from within Africa and outside, and represents the most dramatic evidence for the startling specialization of humans and their widespread radiation to other parts of the globe. This branch of the hominin lineage led to taller, more upright posture, longer leg bones to enhance locomotion, and large cranial capacity. The jaws and back teeth became less massive and more generalized, allowing these emerging humans to eat a wide variety of hard and soft foods. This was in contrast to the so-called robust australopithecines living at the same time—hominins whose skulls and jaws became more muscular, and whose back teeth became larger for the specialized processing of the hardest foods, such as nuts and seeds.

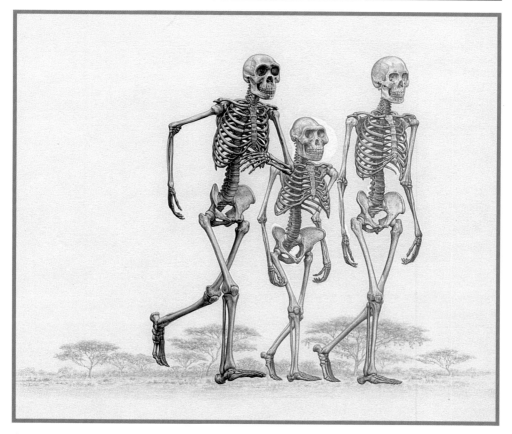

Comparing *H. erectus*, Lucy, and *H. sapiens*

The cranial capacity of *H. erectus* approaches that of modern humans, with an average capacity of 1,000 cc. This is about a third less than the average for *H. sapiens* but twice as large as that of australopithecines. The cranial bones in *H. erectus* were thickened. This is a derived feature found in hominins that results from the natural selection of progressively thicker skull walls for the protection of the increasingly important brain of these species.

There is a trend in *H. erectus* toward smaller teeth and a less prognathic jaw, although all of these features continue to distinguish the *H. erectus* skull from that of modern humans. This hominin showed a continuing trend toward height and bipedalism

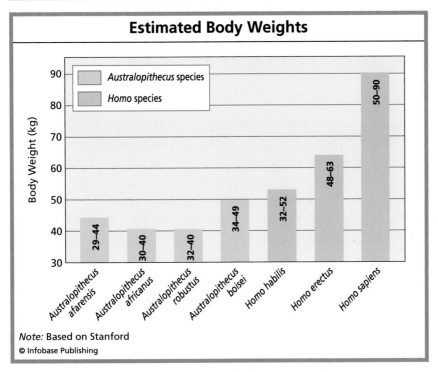

Estimated Body Weights

Legend:
- Australopithecus species
- Homo species

Body Weight (kg) axis: 30, 40, 50, 60, 70, 80, 90

- *Australopithecus afarensis*: 29–44
- *Australopithecus africanus*: 30–40
- *Australopithecus robustus*: 32–40
- *Australopithecus boisei*: 34–49
- *Homo habilis*: 32–52
- *Homo erectus*: 48–63
- *Homo sapiens*: 50–90

Note: Based on Stanford
© Infobase Publishing

Estimated body weights of the early hominins, *Australopithecus* species
(green) and *Homo* spicies (blue)

that equaled, in many respects, the height and erect posture seen in
H. sapiens. With origins as far back as 1.8 million years ago in
Africa, *H. erectus* eventually traveled widely to live in other lands.
Specimens have been found in the Georgian region of central Asia
as well as in China (Peking Man) and Indonesia (Java Man).

Homo antecessor (800,000 to 1.1 million years ago, Spain). The
discovery in 1990 of another species of early hominin moves the
story of the *Homo* radiation to Europe back by about 500,000 years.
H. antecessor is known from the fragmentary fossils of more than
six individuals. These pieces reveal a species that was slightly more
advanced or derived than *H. erectus*. *H. antecessor* stood up to 6 feet

(continues on page 60)

THINK ABOUT IT

The Evolving Brain

One of the most important evolutionary traits of humans is a brain that is dramatically larger than that of humans' African ape relatives. In examinations of fossil hominins, the cranial capacity, measured in cubic centimeters (cc), is a feature often cited to demonstrate the gradual development of larger and larger brains. Interestingly, the first hominin species, such as the australopithecines, did not show the dramatic increase in brain size that is found in later *Homo* species. Although australopithecines' cranial capacity indeed increased over the course of their evolution, it never reached the capacity found in *Homo*.

The large brain of humans is associated with the most recent stages of hominin evolution. When looking at cranial capacity from the fossil record of early *Homo* species, we see that the development of the large brain appears to have occurred rapidly beginning about 1.8 million years ago with *Homo ergaster* and *Homo erectus*. Even early *Homo* species showed dramatically larger brains than australopithecines: The brain of *H. erectus* was twice as large as that of *Australopithecus afarensis*. Australopithecines showed a trend toward a somewhat larger brain. Their most important legacy when it comes to their biological evolution, however, was the innovation of bipedalism.

The accompanying chart illustrates the evolution of increasing cranial capacity in *H. erectus*, comparing it with that of modern humans.

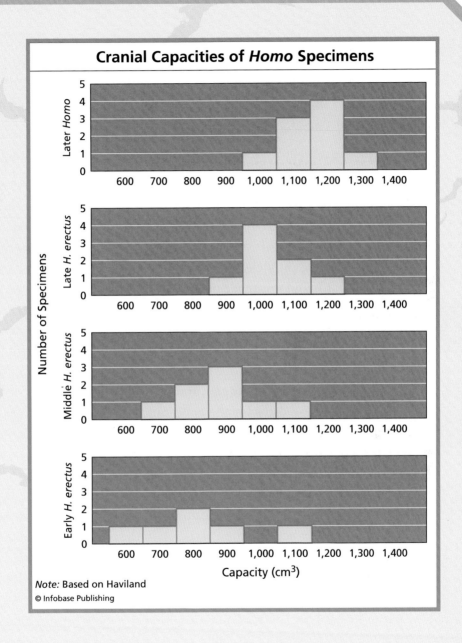

Cranial Capacities of *Homo* Specimens

Note: Based on Haviland

© Infobase Publishing

(continued from page 57)

(1.8 m) tall and had a cranial capacity in slight excess of 1,000 cc. The fossil face of a boy from these finds shows such modern features as a sharp nose and hollowed cheekbones. Other fragments suggest less modern aspects, such as a prominent brow and primitive premolars.

GEOGRAPHIC DISTRIBUTION OF EARLY *HOMO*

Despite the debates over the definitions and lineage of early *Homo* species, it is clear that by about 1.8 million years ago, species of *Homo* had begun to radiate beyond their points of origin in eastern and southern Africa. Fossils associated with *H. erectus* and *H. ergaster* make this abundantly clear. This dispersal was fairly quick by geologic standards and was made possible by land bridges that connected Africa, Europe, Asia, and Indonesia. The earliest *H. erectus* species found in Java date from soon after the dispersal from Africa, about 1.6 million to 1.8 million years ago. Other specimens document the appearance of *Homo* in Europe (900,000 years ago, Italy); central Asia (1.75 million years ago, Georgia); and China (1.8 million years ago).

Based on these dates for the appearance of *H. erectus* in various regions of the world, one might wonder how a species can first appear at about the same time in more than one place. Having widespread fossils dating from about the same time—1.8 million years ago—is not as problematic as may seem, however. First, differing dating methods used to ascertain the age of specimens in Africa, China, and Java might themselves account for a variation in the estimated age of these fossils; such estimates could differ by tens of thousands of years.

Second, it might very well be that the earliest *H. erectus* specimens from Africa are yet to be found or, more likely, never will be found because of the spotty nature of the fossil record. One can assume that *H. erectus* probably arose somewhat earlier in Africa than the officially acknowledged date of 1.8 million years ago.

Finally, even if *H. erectus* did indeed arise in Africa about 1.8 million years ago, it may have taken less than 20,000 years for this population eventually to make its way to Asia on foot, walking the 10,000 to 15,000 miles (16,000 to 24,000 km) from Africa and gradually expanding eastward, generation after generation. While one hopes that this fossil record will be fine-tuned with the discovery of additional specimens, the pattern is fairly clear. *Homo* species—with their improved intelligence, increased mobility, and growing handmade tool technology—found it possible to adapt quickly to a wide range of habitats and food sources.

The reasons for widespread dispersal of early *Homo* may be due to nothing more than *Homo*'s reproductive success. This assumption is loaded with implications, however: What would make these mammals more successful than others, including their australopithecine ancestors? Some reasons for the rapid success and radiation of early *Homo* include the following:

Toolmaking Technology

Until recently, paleoanthropologists assumed that the earliest stone tools were associated with the first known *Homo* species, *H. habilis*, dating from about 2.5 million years ago. In 1999, however, primitive stone tools dating back to about the same time were discovered in association with the australopithecine *A. garhi* (2.5 million years ago, Ethiopia). Although *Homo* species eventually took the making of tools to new levels of sophistication, it appears that at least some species of australopithecines were as capable of making simple tools as the earliest species of *Homo*.

The first stone tools associated with *H. habilis* were found in the Olduvai Gorge area and are known as the Oldowan tool industry. The handmade stone tools from this region were used by *H. habilis* and possibly *Australopithecus robustus*. Two types of primitive Oldowan tools are cutting flakes (for cutting animal hides or scraping meat from bones) and hammer stones (for pounding hard objects such as animal bones or creating new cutting flakes from core stones). The use of tools was an increasingly important adaptive strategy for early humans. It provided them with the means to shape their habitat and circumstances to improve their survival.

There is evidence from the Ivory Coast in Africa that early chimps fashioned nut-cracking hammers out of stone 4,300 years ago. Most tools associated with apes, however, are natural objects such as sticks that have been adapted as tools without the engagement of toolmaking itself. In contract, Oldowan tools required another degree of intellect beyond that of apes: the ability to make a tool from an object that was not naturally found in the form of a tool. The ability to do this implies a degree of imagination, memory, planning, and purpose that apparently was at the heart of the success of early humans. Furthermore, it appears that even the earliest Oldowan toolmakers held onto their tools and carried them from place to place, leaving clues to their presence in numerous locations throughout eastern and southern Africa.

Somewhat later, between 1.4 million and 1.6 million years ago, another tool kit of early humans appears. Called Acheulean tools after a fossil site in France, these were the first stone tools to use bifacial flaking—the process of carefully flaking two sides of a stone to produce a sharp edge, or point, where the edges of the flakes meet. The Acheulean tools apply this superior technology to many of the basic functions found in the older Oldowan tool kit: scrapers, choppers, and cutters. In addition, Acheulean technology could fashion points that were used in hand axes—axes that are held in the hand without a handle.

Acheulean tools are found at many *H. erectus* sites ranging from southern and eastern Africa to Asia and Indonesia. In 1948, after studying the occurrence of tool artifacts including Acheulean tools, American anthropologist Hallam L. Movius (1907–1987) proposed an imaginary line across northern India that marked a difference between the technology found in Africa, Europe, and central Asia and the technology found eastern Asia. To the west of the line were found hand axes and chopping tools; to the east, only chopping tools were found. What is interesting for this discussion is that the so-called Movius Line also represents the widespread migration of Archeulean tools with their respective *H. erectus* toolmakers, a testament to the importance of such tools to the **adaptive radiation** of early humans.

Food Acquisition

An increase in population size eventually would have stretched the food resources available to any group of early humans. While they were adapted well to partake of a variety of foods, from vegetable to animal, the resources of the savanna were not overly abundant. Savanna conditions would have required these hominins to fan out in ever-widening circles to locate food and water. The large brains of *H. erectus* also had a higher **metabolic** cost, making *H. erectus* more needy than its ancestors in the acquisition of high-energy food sources, including animal protein. The need to find more and better food, especially as population numbers grew, would have led naturally to the movement of *Homo* groups across Africa, north to Europe, and east to Asia.

Competition and Social Harmony

Anthropologist Michael Park of Central Connecticut State University points out that increased competition among groups of early humans may have been another reason for their dispersal to greener pastures. The seasonal watering holes that are found in Africa can become dangerous meeting grounds when animals of all kinds find refuge there. A shortage of water is also good enough reason to move from one region to another. Early humans also may have found themselves in competition for living space and shelter with others of their own kind as well as with **predatory** mammals such as big cats. As they wandered out of Africa, early humans found new living spaces, new food sources, and new climates to which they could readily adapt.

OTHER ADAPTATIONS OF ARCHAIC *HOMO* SPECIES

In addition to the toolmaking technology that originated with early *Homo* species, the spread of *H. erectus* to widespread corners of the Old World was accompanied by a number of other innovative adaptations that enhanced the success of *H. erectus* as a species. Along with their fossil bones, early humans left many traces that provide evidence for important behaviors and early cultural practices.

Although we have no idea as to the thinking process of *H. erectus*, these early humans left behind clues to their behavior in the form of **material culture**. Material culture consists of objects and physical evidence left by hominin cultures and found in the fossil record. Such clues often can lead to special insight into the lives of such early people.

Hunting

The activity of hunting does not necessarily require tools; chimps and lions hunt without weapons. Ancestral humans improved their ability to hunt, however, using primitive technology. Stone tools predominated in the toolmaking activities of *H. erectus* well into the middle of the Pleistocene Epoch, a time popularly known as the Stone Age. Along with their Archeulean toolmaking skills, there is evidence that by about 400,000 years ago, early humans were using wooden spears. Together, the technologies of sharp-edged flaked stones, throwing rocks, and wooden weapons provided the means for early humans to hunt and kill game of various sizes. There is evidence supporting this behavior. Whether early humans sought big game animals—and the risks associated with hunting them—is less easy to determine. Certainly, it would have been to the advantage of some populations to find and hunt large animals. Paleoanthropologist Craig Stanford of the University of Southern California suggests that actively hunting big game in northerly climates would have allowed early human populations to better adapt and expand their range into new territories.

Hunting provides insight into the workings of the early human mind. The prospect of hunting requires not only the making of weapons but also foresight, planning, and a systematized approach to attacking prey animals that is learned, first, through trial and error and then, possibly, taught to others.

Some fossil sites contain evidence suggestive of big-game hunting. The aforementioned wooden spears, discovered in a middle Pleistocene fossil locality in Germany, were found in association with the butchered remains of 10 horses and scraping tools for removing flesh from their bones. This is a particularly rare find because although it can be assumed that early *Homo* used wood for a variety of purposes, artifacts made of wood rarely become fossilized. Described by German anthropologist Helmut Thieme in 1997 and dating from 400,000 years ago, the spears are the oldest known completely intact hunting weapons associated with early humans.

Three spears were found, each made by stripping the bark and branches from a narrow spruce sapling and sharpening one end. The spears ranged in size from 6 feet (1.82 m) to 7.4 feet (2.25 m) long. Each was fairly slender; the longest spear had a maximum diameter of 1.9 inches (47 mm) at the thickest point along its shaft. The spears were weighted for throwing, not unlike a javelin. This suggests a stealth hunting style requiring practiced throwing skill. The tips of the spears appear to have been seasoned by firing them—evidence of the controlled use of fire by about 400,000 years ago. In the same fossil-bearing deposit as the spears were found as many as 10,000 bone fragments. These were mainly from horses, and many fragments showed evidence of butchery. The conclusion: The spears were made for hunting large animals.

Middle Pleistocene sites are particularly well preserved in East Africa. The remains of medium- to large-sized mammals frequently are found in association with human campsites. Such sites may have supported as many as 50 people and, according to Milford Wolpoff, contain a number of different tools associated with hunting and with butchering meat. Meat, it would seem, was a regular staple of the hominin diet. Among the tools found at these sites are sharpened flakes used for butchering dead animals and some crude bifacial tools, sometimes with a handle like a pick, that possibly were used for chopping, shredding, and crushing plants and nuts. Hunting implements found at these sites include wooden spears, clubs, and throwing rocks. Animal remains found in the same locations include a variety of mammals, among them giant baboons.

A hominin site found in England dates from about 500,000 years ago and includes stone tools and axes in association with a variety of large mammal remains, including rhinoceroses.

Although organized hunting appears to have been a practice of early humans, there is also evidence that they were active scavengers. Bones of prey animals found at human fossil sites often show such signs of butchering as evidence of the use of flake tools to scrape meat from bones. Paleoanthropologist Pat Shipman of Pennsylvania State University used the power of the electron microscope to examine many of these sample remains more closely. What she found was a consistent pattern of tool cuts overlying tooth marks from other predatory animals. This evidence strongly suggests that humans were active scavengers as well as hunters and often stole the kills of other animals in whole or in part for their own consumption. The humans may have waited for predators to leave the scene or may have frightened them away temporarily, just long enough to rip off part of the carcass. The humans then took their scavenged meat back to their safe haven, such as a cave, where the meat could be butchered for the group to consume.

Based on this abundance of evidence regarding hunting, scavenging, and the presence of a wide range of tools at hominin sites, paleoanthropologist Philip Stein concludes that early humans were predominantly scavengers and plant gatherers but would hunt if the need or opportunity presented itself.

Harnessing Fire

Homo erectus probably was the first human species to introduce the controlled use of fire. Fire was familiar to early humans as a natural phenomenon caused by lightning strikes or the spontaneous combustion of wildfires by hot volcanic ash. It is surmised that early humans may have captured such fire and brought it back to camp to form a protective barrier against night creatures or simply to manufacture warmth. The management of fire, its creation, and its control would have given early cultures new powers over their lives. Anthropologist Christopher Stringer of the Natural History Museum in London suggests that fire would have encouraged early people to gather together around a campfire, enriching their social lives.

Although there is some evidence for the presence of fire at hominin sites going back as far as 1.5 million years in East Africa, it is not clear whether early humans created these fires. One example comes from South Africa and dates from about 1 million to 1.5 million years ago. A number of burned bones were found in the

Swartkrans cave, known for its abundant remains of *Australopithecus* specimens. Although there is no evidence that hominins started the fire that burned the bones, chemical tests have shown that these specimens were burned at a temperature that corresponds to that of a hot campfire.

The best evidence for the harnessing of fire comes from fossil sites that date from between 300,000 and 500,000 million years ago in France, Spain, Hungary, and Asia. This evidence consists of charred bones and ashes but no actual hearths built to contain a fire.

Fire is of interest because it adds to the repertoire of early human adaptations for sustaining life. Cooking is not just a luxury that changes the taste of meat. Cooking preserves meat longer than would be the case if it were raw. Fire also is an essential component of warming a shelter in a cold environment—another talent that may have improved the mobility of early humans into more northerly climates.

Shelters

The preponderance of *H. erectus* evidence shows that these early humans may have taken shelter in caves. There is little evidence in the fossil record regarding temporary shelters that they may have constructed outside of such naturally protective gathering places, however. Caves would have provided an excellent barrier against outside predators. Caves also would have offered shelter from weather and improved the ability to use fire to keep the group warm. It is fair to assume that early humans built temporary campsites outside, an assumption made even more plausible by their growing capacity to devise and make tools. Hard evidence of temporary shelters, however, will be difficult to find in the fossil record.

A significant fossil location providing evidence of prehistoric shelters is Terra Amata in France, near Nice. The sites contains a series of shallow dwellings and living floors dating back as far as 380,000 years, making them the earliest evidence of human dwellings. The living floors contain stone artifacts that some paleoanthropologists interpret as representing supports for what were probably hut walls made of wooden poles. Not everyone agrees on this interpretation because the living floors most likely contain an accumulation of artifacts from many sedimentary layers of earth that covered the location over time. There is little dispute, however, that Terra Armata represents an early human living site of some sort. The site contains many stone tools, animal bones, and traces of fossilized human feces. Terra Amata was probably a killing site where animals were butchered.

A PHYLOGENY OF EARLY *HOMO*

Understanding the family tree of *Homo* is a hotly debated issue in paleoanthropology. Such disagreement among scientists is not uncommon, however, when the availability of data continues to increase year after year, as it does in the study of early humans. The practice of science is all about asking questions, clarifying once-cloudy details, and detecting and correcting error. In this regard, the continuing discovery of early human fossils provides much needed data in a field in which the odds of finding adequate information are stacked against the scientist. A bounty of discoveries during the past 15 years has outpaced the ability of the scientific community to fully absorb the new data. This is an excellent problem to have, but having so much information also makes the picture of human evolution increasingly complex to interpret.

In Chapter 1 we recalled the words of paleoanthropologist John Fleagle, who reminded us that the features that define human beings "are not necessarily linked but rather evolved one by one." A century ago, the quest for the "missing link" suggested a simple, straight-line evolutionary path from the great apes to *Homo*. The hoax of the Piltdown Man specimen was the self-fulfilling prophecy of at least one clique of paleonanthropologists who wanted it to be true. That straight-line story line began to fall apart, however, as early human specimens began to crop up in such far-flung places as eastern and southern Africa, Europe, Central Asia, China, and Indonesia. Every new published report of a fossil hominin has the potential to modify our understanding of human evolution. The availability of more fossil data improves the ability to work out the phylogeny—the ancestral relationships—of extinct human species, but the availability of more data also leads to different opinions. It is important to view any proposed phylogeny of humans as tentative—a mere snapshot in time based on currently available information.

Many of the disagreements regarding the phylogeny of ancestral humans revolve around the definition of given species. We have described some species of *Australopithecus* and *Homo* for which there is much disagreement. Were *H. ergaster* and *H. erectus* two separate species or one and the same? Was *A. robustus* actually a separate species that some call *Paranthropous robustus*? These examples represent two generalized approaches to classifying hominins that go by the names *lumpers* and *splitters.*

Lumpers are paleoanthropologists who focus on the similarities among specimens rather than on the differences. By doing this, lumpers tend to recognize the widespread diversity within a population for the purpose of "lumping" most specimens into one taxon. This approach to classifying a taxon will serve lumpers well until good-enough evidence presents itself to warrant the recognition of a new species. Lumpers will group all specimens of *Australopithecus* into a single taxon rather than divide them into other species that have been suggested, such as *Paranthropus*. An extreme case of lumping in the study of *Homo* is the consideration of only a single species—that of *Homo sapiens*. In the lumpers' view of human evolution, every ancestor of modern humans is merely an archaic *H. sapiens*.

Splitters are paleoanthropologists who tend to focus on the differences between fossil specimens and will assign specimens to different taxa based on such differences. Differences that are considered minor may result in the assignment of new species within a given genus. Differences that are considered major—such as a modification of the dental battery—may result in the naming of a new genus for a given taxon. In the case of the evolution of modern humans, splitters recognize seven or more species of archaic *Homo* leading to *H. sapiens*.

Using a lumping or splitting approach to classifying early humans is merely a starting point for putting the pieces of the evolutionary puzzle together. As paleoanthropologist Michael Park points out, "no researcher is always a splitter or lumper." Likewise, any good scientist will acknowledge new data that might modify his or her scheme, continuing the incremental clarification of facts that is at the heart of scientific research.

Debating the validity of the lumper and splitter points of view is not a goal of this book. The two approaches are presented here by way of showing the kinds of issues faced by scientists in their day-to-day research. What is of most interest in this book is the overall picture of hominin evolution revealed by the many discoveries of fossil humans discussed in these pages. For the purposes of this discussion, this book has focused on the most widely recognized species of early humans for which there is a preponderance of evidence. These include, as you have seen, a number of early species of *Homo*.

Chapter 3 discusses the most recent evolution of *Homo* and the emergence of the species *H. sapiens* during the past 200,000 years.

SUMMARY

This chapter traced the discoveries of early *Homo*, described key specimens, and discussed problems of establishing evolutionary links between modern *Homo* and ancestral humans.

1. Early hominins become candidates for the genus *Homo* when their anatomical features more closely resemble those seen in modern humans than they resemble the features seen in australopithecines.

2. The earliest discoveries of early *Homo* species of great significance were in Asia. These included such historic finds as Java Man and Peking Man, later resolved as specimens of *Homo erectus*. These discoveries initially diverted the search for the earliest human ancestors to Asia.

3. The earliest known *Homo* species is that of *Homo habilis*, discovered by Louis and Mary Leakey and named in 1964. The presence of *H. habilis* in East Africa confirmed the African origins of ancestral humans.

4. Specimens of *Homo erectus*, widely found throughout Africa, Europe, and Asia, represent several adaptive specializations leading to modern humans. These adaptations include a taller, more upright posture; longer leg bones to enhance locomotion; and large cranial capacity.

5. By about 1.8 million years ago, species of *Homo* began to radiate beyond their points of origin in eastern and southern Africa.

6. Reasons considered for the widespread geographic distribution of early humans include reproductive success, advanced adaptive technology such as tools, increasing demands on the availability of natural resources such as food, and competition with other populations of ancestral humans.

7. Other adaptations associated with early *Homo* species include hunting, the management of fire, and the likely construction of shelters.

8. Despite its often-fragmentary nature, there is a wealth of known fossil material for early humans. Much of this fossil material is newly discovered, having been found in the past 15 years.

9. The availability of more fossil data improves the ability to work out the phylogeny of extinct human species, but it also leads to different opinions.

10. Lumpers are paleoanthropologists who focus on the similarities among specimens rather than on the differences. Splitters are paleoanthropologists who tend to focus on the differences between fossil specimens and will assign specimens to different taxa based on such differences.

SECTION TWO:
MODERN HUMANS

3

PREMODERN HUMANS OF THE GENUS *HOMO*

The Pleistocene Epoch began about 1.8 million years ago and lasted until about 10,000 years ago. The evolution, diversification, and geographic radiation of early *Homo* species began at about the Pliocene-Pleistocene boundary and expanded dramatically. By about the end of the Pliocene, the species *Homo* appears to have split off from ancestral australopithecine stock, possibly as *H. erectus*, and the last remaining species of *Australopithecus* became extinct.

Chapter 2 discussed the diversity of early *Homo* species during the first million years or so of their evolution. This chapter examines the most recent *Homo* species to emerge during the past 500,000 years, just prior to and alongside the rise of modern humans in the form of *Homo sapiens*. Among these now-lost human species are the *H. neanderthalensis*, or Neandertals—the best known early peoples other than *H. sapiens*—as well as *H. heidelbergensis* from Germany and *H. floresiensis* from Indonesia, the so-called "hobbit" species.

CLIMATE, GEOLOGY, AND EARLY HOMO EVOLUTION

The Pleistocene Epoch is also called the Ice Age because during this time, large masses of ice advanced and retreated periodically, primarily in the Northern Hemisphere. Earth has been affected by similar ice ages throughout its history, but the Pleistocene is the most recent and the only one to affect the human species directly.

During an ice age, during spans called **glacial** periods, ice advances over large areas of land. During a glacial period, worldwide temperatures cool and sea levels drop as a large portion of ocean water freezes. At no time during a glacial period does the advancing ice cover the entire planet. In the Pleistocene, large portions of North America, Europe, and Asia were covered in ice. Antarctica, too, experienced increased glaciation during these times. Many parts of Earth above and below the equator were not covered in ice, however.

Glacial periods were followed by **interglacial** periods of warming, during which ice retreated somewhat for another long span of time. The average global temperatures during the interglacial periods of the Pleistocene often were warmer than today. This cycle of colder and warmer climates was repeated many times during the Pleistocene. Paleoanthropologist Ian Tattersall of the American Museum of Natural History has been able to document 15 periods of major glaciation and as many as 50 minor encroaches of ice during the Pleistocene Ice Age in Europe alone. The most recent glacial episode drew to a close around 10,000 years ago. We currently are experiencing what appears to be an interglacial episode.

The Ice Age naturally affected the course of life on Earth. When glaciers retreated, forests spread. When glaciers were in full force in the northern hemisphere, the climate of Africa became more arid because of less rainfall, and the deserts of northern Africa expanded widely. During interglacial periods, desert sands turned into grassy savannas and once-dwindling wooded areas reclaimed the center of the continent in the form of succulent rain forests.

The changing environments of the Pleistocene naturally affected human evolution. The cycle of glaciation during the Pleistocene waxed and waned on a 100,000-year rhythm. Plant and animal food sources changed over time, requiring humans to adapt different sustenance strategies. Glacial periods had two consequences for the migration patterns of humans and other mammals. When the sands of northern Africa expanded across the width of the continent, the inhospitable environment effectively blocked any passage from southern Africa to Europe. In the northern hemisphere, as glaciers advanced, shallow seas froze and land bridges formed that permitted the migration of humans and other animals to adjoining landmasses. One such connection linked Asia and North America.

The fossil record of the past million years was greatly affected by the periodic effects of advancing and receding glaciers. Vertebrate fossils are found mostly in **sedimentary** rock layers—deposits of earth and rock that become layered, are compressed, and harden over time to form rocks. These rock layers contain the bones of creatures that died in the mud or dirt of ancient times. The movement of glaciers rips apart the earthen crust beneath these rocks, gouging out sedimentary layers and the fossils that they contain. Most such hijacked remains disintegrate after they are freed from the rock in which they were contained, although in some cases, the fossils might survive long enough to be deposited elsewhere. Such isolated fossils lose much of their innate value because they have been removed not only from the informative sedimentary context in which they were created, but also from other parts of the same specimen that might convey more complete data about the given organism. Radioactive and chemical methods can be used on some fossils to date them accurately, but knowing where such fossils originated is not easy to decipher. Generally speaking, human fossils from the middle to late Pleistocene are few and far between. Many of the best specimens have been found in cave environments that were unaffected by glaciers and were left abandoned or were naturally obstructed long ago.

The *Homo* species discussed in this chapter lived from the middle to the end of the Pleistocene, during the most recent period of glaciation. Some paleoanthropologists call these species "presapiens," meaning that collectively they represent an adaptive radiation of *Homo* species prior to the emergence of anatomically modern humans. From the standpoint of evolutionary relationships between species, we assume that all *Homo* species have a common ancestor. The identification of this ancestor is still one of the most hotly debated issues in paleoanthropology, however. As indicated in Chapter 2, based on current evidence—evidence that is admittedly sketchy—many scientists feel that _H. erectus_ currently is the most likely candidate for the common ancestor of _Homo_ species.

HOMO HEIDELBERGENSIS

The first specimen of _Homo heidelbergensis_ consisted of a lower jaw with teeth. It was found near Heidelberg, Germany, in 1907. The name is now used to refer to several widespread specimens found throughout the Old World, from Africa to Europe and Asia. In comparison with _H. erectus_, _H. heidelbergensis_ had a somewhat more modern skull, with a higher forehead and larger cranial capacity. By some measures, the cranial capacity of _H. heidelbergensis_ was as much as 30 percent larger than the capacity of earlier _Homo_ species and fell within the range of modern humans.

Other traits of the skull show signs of modernism as well. These traits include a smaller face, a jaw that juts less than that of _H. erectus,_ a somewhat reduced brow, and somewhat reduced thickness in the temple area. Other features, though, clearly show that _H. heidelbergensis_ was not quite modern. These include its receding chin, its less domelike cranium, and its limb bones that are still much thicker and heavier, when viewed in cross section, than the limbs of _H. sapiens._

Specimens from three continents have been assigned to the taxon _H. heidelbergensis_ and span a time frame of about 400,000 years. A collection of bones including a skull, upper jaw, pelvis, and other postcranial elements was found in Zambia between 1921 and 1925. These fossils were dated to about 300,000 years ago. Despite the nearly modern cranial capacity of 1,280 cc of these Zambian skulls, the specimens possess the thick brow ridges that usually are associated with older species. The brow was also low and sloped and the skull more rounded than that of _H. erectus._

Another skull assigned to _H. heidelbergensis_ was found in Ethiopia. It dates from 600,000 years ago and is quite similar to the Zambia specimen except for its much older date.

A scattering of finds from Europe also has been assigned to _H. heidelbergensis._ These finds include fragmentary skulls and limb

An artist's interpretation of
H. heidelbergensis

elements from England, Hungary, Germany, Greece, and France. These materials have been collected since 1933 and represent hominins that lived from about 200,000 to 525,000 years ago, a time span roughly similar to that of the finds from Africa that have been associated with *H. heidelbergensis*. The most informative of these specimens is the skull from Germany, which has a combination of primitive and more derived traits. This skull features a primitive sloping forehead and large brows, but its face is smaller, its jaw is not prognathic, and its teeth are relatively small.

Fragmentary remains from China include two badly crushed skulls with faces from Yunxian in central China. Dated to about 500,000 to 600,000 years ago, the skulls have flatter, broader faces than those seen in the specimens of *H. heidelbergensis* from Europe and Africa. It is not widely agreed that these archaic *Homo* skulls from Yunxian are, in fact, related to *H. heidelbergensis*. Some scientists argue, rather, that they are another branch of the presapien lineage that developed in Asia.

HOMO NEANDERTHALENSIS

If by chance you happen to strike up a conversation with some friends about human origins, you probably will elicit some blank stares if you attempt to pepper the conversation with taxon names such as *Australopithecus* and *Homo erectus*. Mention "Neandertals" or "cave people," however, and your listeners will claim to know exactly what it is you are jabbering about. Almost everyone equates the name Neandertal—previously spelled "Neanderthal," before the German language officially dropped the silent "h" from most words about 100 years ago—with a kind of obsolete and brutish ape-man, presumably a "missing link" that bridged the gap between modern people and their ape ancestors.

The name Neandertal has strong connotations, and you would not want to be called one. In popular usage, the name implies a sub-human condition, a failed experiment in evolution, and a stooping brute of a person with hunched shoulders, a hairy body, and apelike features. Because you have come this far with me, however, I trust that such irony is not lost on you. For Neandertals were none of the above.

The Neandertals' proper name is *Homo neanderthalensis*, although during this discussion, we also may call them Neandertals. They are a species of *Homo* that arose in Europe about 200,000 years ago, became widespread throughout Europe and western Asia by about 120,000 years ago, and became extinct only 25,000 years ago. The name Neandertal comes from the Neander Valley near Düsseldorf, Germany, where some of the first specimens were found, in 1856. Apart from anatomically modern humans (see Chapter 4), we understand more about *H. neanderthalensis* than we do about any other extinct hominin species. The remains of Neandertals often are found in association with caves that include tool artifacts, animal bones, and other clues to the Neandertal lifestyle.

H. neanderthalensis is not a "missing link" in any sense of the word. Not only do Neandertals postdate the divergence of hominins from the great apes by a couple of million years, Neandertals were an entirely separate *Homo* species. There is still some question, however, as to whether it was possible for Neandertals and early *Homo sapiens* to interbreed, a debate that figures largely in the question of the way in which early human populations spread across the globe (see Chapter 4). The status of Neandertals as a separate species has not always been widely agreed on. The preponderance of fossil evidence in support of this theory recently has been supported by a comparison of the *H. neanderthalensis* and *H. sapiens* genomes, however, thus proving once and for all the standing of Neandertals as a kind of *Homo* separate from all others.

The status of *H. neanderthalensis* as a separate species also puts to rest the popular misconception that modern humans are descendants of Neandertals. This is not the case. It is best not to confuse the two because, as Ian Tattersall explains, "whatever Neandertal lifestyles were, they were foreign to our own." Yet the Neandertals adapted successfully to climate changes and other obstacles in their path for tens of thousands of years.

The origins of Neandertals are not well understood. Their presence in Europe is well documented, especially within the past 100,000 years. Some of the earliest proto-Neandertal remains date from about 300,000 years again in Spain. Prior to that, not much is known. This lack of data is largely an artifact of the fossil record in Europe, which was wiped clean to some extent by glacial activity. What is known is that Neandertals were widespread but isolated in Europe, the Middle East, and Central Asia. They represent a split from the lineage of later hominins that later led to the speciation of *H. sapiens*. Recent **DNA** analysis and the development of a Neandertal genome by paleoanthropologist Richard E. Green of the Max Planck Institute for Evolutionary Anthropology and colleagues suggest that the lineages leading to modern humans and *H. neanderthalensis* originally split from a common ancestral line about 500,000 years ago.

Anatomical Traits of *H. neanderthalensis*

Neandertals were superficially similar to modern humans. If they were alive today, one might have difficulty telling them from *H. sapiens*. A closer look at their skeletal features, however, reveals many derived features of their skulls and postcranial anatomy that clearly distinguish *H. neanderthalensis* from *H. sapiens*.

The Neandertal skull is large, with a low forehead and a cranial chamber that forms a large, low cranium. The cranial capacity of Neandertals was, on average, as large as that of modern humans, at about 1,400 cc. There is no evidence to show that *H. neanderthalensis* was as smart as *H. sapiens*; this is largely because of the structure of the brain. The brain of modern humans has more space dedicated to functions such as higher thought, spatial reasoning, and language.

In comparison with modern humans, Neandertals had large, rounded eye sockets; a prominent, continuous brow ridge; a wide and high nose; large front teeth; backward sloping cheekbones; and a small, rounded bulge on the back of the cranium. Neandertals' teeth projected forward, and the face was much more prognathic than that of *H. sapiens*. The chin of Neandertals shows a lot of variation, from being weak and receding to having an appearance more like that of modern humans.

The postcranial skeleton of *H. neanderthalensis* features many subtle but important differences when compared with modern humans. If *H. sapiens* were thought of as a passenger car, *H. neanderthalensis* would be the off-road version with somewhat thicker, rigid, and heavy-duty components. The ribs of *H. neanderthalensis* are wide, giving the abdomen a more barrel-like shape. The forearms are surprisingly short, the knees and ankles are thick jointed, and the feet are equipped with wide and strong toes. The shoulders of *H. neanderthalensis* are broader than those of modern humans, and the limb bones generally are thicker and heavier in their composition. The hands and fingers were robust and capable of a mighty grip. In comparing *H. neanderthalensis* with modern humans, it is fair to conclude that the former were more muscular, stronger, and agile enough to handle themselves quite well. The early modern humans that encountered *H. neanderthalensis* were no doubt lighter on their feet and smarter than *H. neanderthalensis* but surely would have lost most arm-wrestling contests with their hominin neighbors.

Neandertal Technology

The tools of early African *Homo* species were described in Chapter 2. They included the simple stone tools known from the Oldowan tool kit dating from about 1.8 million years ago. Oldowan tools included cutting flakes (for cutting animal hides or scraping meat from bones) and hammer stones (for pounding hard objects). Somewhat later, between 1.4 million and 1.6 million years ago, the Acheulean tool kit appeared. These were the first stone tools to use bifacial flaking to create an improved repertoire of scrapers, choppers, and cutters with the same functions as Oldowan tools.

By about 200,000 to 300,000 years ago, there is fossil evidence for an improved variation on the Oldowan and Acheulean toolmaking techniques found first in Africa and then in Europe. Called the Levallois technique, after a district outside Paris where it first was scientifically understood, this toolmaking method is a prepared core technology. In prepared cored technology, a stone is specially selected and then used to make multiple flake tools. It involves the creation of more than one flake of a given size and shape from a single stone core, usually from a material such as flint that is at once hard, easy to flake, and capable of making a sharp edge. The flakes themselves were individual tools used for cutting, scraping, or other common tasks. Levallois technology produced more tools per core, an improvement over Acheulean technology. Neandertals probably were responsible for creating this improved Stone Age technology. Neandertals continued to perfect the Levallois technique, producing a variety of specialized tools, some of which were more difficult to make than others.

Paleoanthropologist Clifford Jolly (b. 1939) of New York University identified several categories of Neandertal tools that were more advanced than tools made with the earlier Oldowan and Acheulean technologies.

Mousterian Point and Tools

The term *Mousterian*, named for a Neandertal fossil site in France, more broadly refers to a late Pleistocene culture that ranged across Europe, North Africa, and western Asia during the start of the most recent glacial period, about 70,000 years ago. Tools made during this time show advanced Levallois technology and sometimes are referred to as having been made with Mousterian technology. The

Mousterian point is a triangular, sharpened stone. It may have been used as a spearhead. Other Mousterian tools include:

Burin. This was a gouging tool that worked like a chisel and was used to shave or shape wood.

Borer. This was a stone with a small point that was used to punch holes in leather.

Denticulate. This was a hand tool with a single rough or serrated edge; it probably was used to shred vegetation.

Notch. This was a small, rounded stone with a notch, probably for attachment to a pole or spear.

Backed knife. This was a long piece of flint with a sharp edge and a grip to protect the hand and provide a firm grasp.

Scraper. This was a thick flake of flint retouched by additional edging to provide a durable tool for scraping meat from bones.

Jolly notes that these tools are found in many varieties, thus showing that Neandertals had developed many specialized applications for stone technology. "Their precise workmanship and repeated production of the same forms," remarks Jolly, are indicative of advancing technology and the ability of the Neandertal stoneworker to learn a tool pattern and repeat it time and time again.

Neandertal Culture

The culture of a hominin groups comprises the accumulation of acquired and learned behaviors shared by member of the population. The concept of accumulated culture is important because it demonstrates a means by which a group passes along its knowledge to the next generation to further the survival of the species.

The culture of ancestral humans comprised elements of technology, as discussed above; the founding of shelters and settlements; subsistence practices to feed the group; symbolic behavior such as language; and other practices, such as burials.

Settlements and Shelters

There is not hard and fast evidence of the size of Neandertal communities, but the fossil record has been kind enough to leave behind some clues as to where and how they might have lived. While some Neandertal groups lived in caves, there is also evidence that others established shelters in open spaces and among natural formations protected by rock walls. Because some of this evidence dates from a period of glaciation, Neandertals surely must have constructed temporary shelters to protect them from the cold and harsh conditions of the Ice Age tundra.

While most evidence for Neandertal shelters in Europe was almost certainly destroyed by the movement of glaciers, at least one intriguing find in the Ukraine offers some clues to the shelter created by one group. Artifacts found at the site, in a location that once was an open space, include an oval ring of mammoth bones that is 26 feet (7.8 m) wide at its broadest point. Within the ring are a variety of tools, waste bones from meals, and charred remains from six or more campfires. It has been surmised that the mammoth bones formed the perimeter of a hut, holding down the edges of animal skins that were stretched out over the ring using wooden poles. This evidence stands as one of the only clear signs that Neandertals sometimes created temporary shelters. Just how many of these shelters there may have been in a community, how long they stayed there, and how many individuals occupied the area is unknown.

Some aspects of Neandertal social behavior also can be extracted from evidence of their shelters. Neandertals did not appear to invest much effort in organizing their living spaces or creating zones for particular kinds of activities, other than to toss bones into a heap. In the case of fire hearths, there often appear to be more than one at Neandertal cave and dwelling sites, and the locations of campfires do not appear to be planned by modern human standards. This is not to fault Neandertals for being disorganized. What appears to be sloppy to us might have made sense to them. We are reminded of Tattersall, who advises against trying to judge Neandertals as if they were just a step on the path to modern humanity. They were not.

A drawing of a Neandertal group

Subsistence Practices and Hunting

The accumulation of animal bones at Neandertal sites clearly shows that they ate meat. While scavenging dead animals may have been a part of their subsistence culture, it is generally agreed that Neandertals also were active hunters. The animal remains found at some sites are impressive. In Crimea, the bones of 287 individual wild asses have been found among Neandertals. The remains of as many as 1,200 bison are associated with a Neandertal group in Hungary. Other sites across the span of the late Pleistocene provide evidence that *H. neanderthalensis* was equally adept at hunting woolly mammoths, bovines, reindeer, rhinoceroses, boar, elk, and horses.

The weapons associated with Neandertals do not include what could be called long-range implements, such as bows and arrows and spear-throwing devices created somewhat later by anatomically modern humans. Neandertals appear to have hunted at close range, using spears, axes, cutting blades, rocks, and wooden clubs.

When and how they hunted is difficult to ascertain from the fossil record, but some clues provide likely scenarios. The presence, for example, of large animal bones among Neandertal remains provides clues to the processing and consumption of animal food. The Neandertal site known as Salzgitter Lebenstedt in Germany is well known for its accumulation of well-preserved reindeer remains. It is one of the most northerly Neandertal sites and represents an arctic setting. Analysis of the reindeer remains suggests several things about the hunting behavior of these Neandertals. In 2000, paleoanthropologists Sabine Gaudzinki of the Römisch-Germanisches Zentralmuseum in Neuwied, Germany, and Wil Roebroeks of Leiden University showed that the selection of adult reindeers indicated an autumn hunt. Once the animals were killed, the carcasses were butchered, and special attention was given to extracting marrow from the bones. This evidence suggests a systematic routine for processing game.

Another intriguing piece of evidence suggests that Neandertals sometimes may have conducted mass kills of prey-animal herds. The French fossil site of Combe-Grenal includes a large number of horse remains. Analysis of the assumed ages of the animals closely matches the ages found in active herds. This suggests that an entire herd may have been killed at one time, possibly swept over a cliff by a group of Neandertals working together.

Although there is little evidence of food other than meat at Neandertal sites, it is assumed that these hominins had a diet that varied as much as the diets of later, better understood **hunter-gatherers**. Neandertals probably added fruits, berries, nuts, and other vegetation to their diets as the seasons allowed.

Language

Language is one of the most fundamental behaviors of modern humans. Can the same be assumed for Neandertals? After all, the *H. neanderthalensis* brain was as large as that of modern humans. The topic of Neandertal language has been a controversial one for many years. Anatomically, the ability to create many vocal sounds

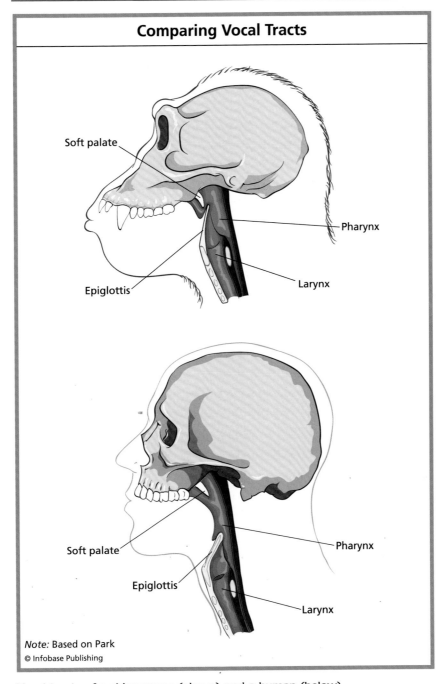

Comparing Vocal Tracts

Soft palate

Pharynx

Epiglottis

Larynx

Soft palate

Pharynx

Epiglottis

Larynx

Note: Based on Park
© Infobase Publishing

Vocal tracts of a chimpanzee (above) and a human (below)

with distinctive differences is a function of the vocal tract. Chimpanzees, for example, are incapable of making the variety of sounds made by humans because chimps' vocalizing equipment—including the pharynx and larynx—are positioned much higher in the throat than in humans. Neandertals, it appears, had a vocal tract similar to that of modern humans. Thus, from an anatomical point of view, Neandertals should have been able to make a wide variety of distinctive sounds, including vowels.

Whether or not the Neandertal brain was equipped for spoken language is another consideration, however. Like modern humans, Neandertals had a brain that was divided into two hemispheres, each of which was wired to communicate and function with the other. Unlike the brains of most other mammals, in which one side duplicates the other as a safeguard against injury—a backup system, if you will—hominin brains gave up redundancy and used the additional capacity to expand their cognitive abilities. The language center of the modern human brain is not clearly visible in an endocast. An endocast of a hominin skull can provide only clues to the size, connections, and outside surface of the brain that once was inside that skull and so can provide no visual evidence to the presence of a language center in the Neandertal brain. Scientists who study the endocasts of Neandertal brains are quick to point out, however, that the outward size, shape, and neural connections of the *H. neanderthalensis* brain cannot be distinguished from those of living humans. Neandertals therefore appear to have had the anatomy and brain functions to engage in articulate speech.

Another clue to solving the puzzle of Neandertal language comes from recent genomic studies of modern humans and Neandertals. The detection of a "language gene" may hold a clue to the first appearance of language in hominins. In 2002, a research team headed by Wolfgang Enard of the Max Planck Institute for Evolutionary Anthropology conducted a study of the DNA of a family in which half the members are severely impaired when it comes to their linguistic, grammatical, and articulation skills. The team was able to identify DNA whose encoding appears to be responsible for helping humans articulate language and that is absent in the most closely related great apes. Once introduced, a genomic variation such as this would have selectively radiated throughout human populations, eventually spreading to all humankind. In fact, the team sampled DNA from living humans on all continents and found the so-called "language gene" present in every case.

So far, this is the only gene implicated in human speech function. This makes this gene a likely target for further study in the possible genetic makeup of ancestral humans.

Could Neanderthals speak? Did they possess the language gene identified by the Max Planck researchers? The picture became much clearer in 2007, with the availability of the first completed Neandertal genome. The same language gene was found in Neandertal samples. Because Neandertals were a species distinct from modern humans, it appears that the genetic ability to articulate speech was in the DNA of hominins prior to the split between Neandertals and those species that included modern human ancestors.

The conclusion, then, is that Neandertals had the means and ability to develop spoken language. Whether they did so is unknown, however. Some researchers regard the flowering of language as only influencing the success of modern humans. As such, the development of language in *H. sapiens* may have been a part of a combination of behaviors unseen, unneeded, or simply undeveloped in Neandertals.

Burials

Neandertals deliberately buried their dead. Some well-known fossil sites consist primarily of burial remains and serve as some of the best evidence of Neandertal anatomy. The oldest evidence of burial is located in Israel and dates from 90,000 years ago. The cave of Kaprina in Croatia, dating from about 70,000 years ago, contained the remains of 43 individuals, the greatest number of any Neandertal site. The Iraqi site at Shanidar cave contained 9 individuals buried between 40,000 and 50,000 years ago. At least 12 individuals were buried at the site in La Ferrassie, France, which dates from 35,000 years ago.

Neandertal burial sites differ from those of the earliest modern humans in several respects. All Neandertal sites are found in caves, whereas some early *H. sapiens* burial sites are located in open areas. For the most part, Neandertal burial sites also are unadorned, and although about half of these sites contains miscellaneous objects inside the graves, there is no agreement that these objects were placed there intentionally as grave goods. In many cases of Neandertal burials, the bodies were bent in a flexed posture rather than being laid out fully extended.

Paleoanthropologists caution not to read too much into Neandertal burials. A modern view of the world would assume that burial practices are always associated with religious beliefs, but this is not likely the case at all with Neandertals. Were they honoring their dead or paying them respect by burying them? Perhaps there was a more practical reason, such as the disposal of a rotting corpse, either for sanitary reasons or to hide the remains from dangerous predators that otherwise might be attracted by the smell of the body. One Neandertal site in Spain contains the remains of 28 individuals whose bodies apparently were hurled down a vertical shaft for disposal.

Arts

There is some evidence that Neandertals made art objects for personal adornment. The making of art is a form of symbolic behavior that is clearly associated with later humans. The skillful making of stone tools was certainly a craft employed by Neandertals, and there are examples of decorated objects made by Neandertals, some dating back 100,000 years or more. These objects generally include engraved or tooled bones and teeth. Examples include holes drilled in small, beadlike teeth and parallel lines or zigzag patterns etched on bones. Evidence of cave paintings, so prevalent in the caves of early modern humans, is not found at Neandertal sites.

HOMO FLORESIENSIS

A previously unknown species of extinct *Homo* came to light in 2003. Paleoanthropologists Peter Brown of the University of New England in New South Wales, Australia, and Thomas Sutikna of the Indonesian Centre for Archaeology, Jakarta, led a team of workers to the Indonesian island of Flores in search of archaeological clues to the migration of early *H. sapiens* from Asia to Australia. Instead, the team was surprised to discover fossils belonging to a very small hominin. At first, the team was not certain that the specimen belonged to a previously unknown species of hominin or merely represented an example of some pathologic disorder among modern humans. The finding of additional fossil material since 2003 and various studies by the team and other researchers now confirm that this small hominin was actually part of a separate species of *Homo*. It has been given the name *Homo floresiensis* after the island on which it was found.

H. floresiensis is known from a small but significant set of fossil remains, including a cranium and mandible and such postcranial elements as parts of limbs, ribs, shoulder fragments, parts of the pelvis, vertebrae, and partial hands and feet. As many as eight individuals are represented by these remains, and all exhibit the same degree of dwarfism. The average height of *H. floresiensis* was slightly more than 3.5 feet (1.8 m). This is shorter than the average height of the smallest known examples of modern humans, such as African and Malaysian "pygmies," who range between 4.5 and 4.9 feet (1.35 and 1.47 m) tall.

In addition to height, several other anatomical features clearly separate *H. floresiensis* from *H. sapiens*. *H. floresiensis* appears to comprise a combination of primitive and derived features not seen in other hominins, thus fortifying its stature as a separate species. Its cranial capacity is about the same as that of the australopithecines when viewed as a proportion of body weight. *H. floresiensis* does not possess the jutting jaw and oversized tooth batteries of those ancestral humans, however. Instead, the dental plan, skull shape and size, and posture appear to be quite modern—factors that enable this species to be assigned to the genus *Homo*. Other primitive features of *H. floresiensis* include a receding chin, robust leg bones, and long arms that are more like those of australopithecines than those of modern humans.

Specimens of *H. floresiensis* span a time frame from 18,000 to 38,000 years ago. Two jawbones that were found are virtually identical, even though they date from about 3,000 years apart. This is another indication that these bones belonged to an established species rather than to individuals suffering from some form of pathologically caused dwarfism that would not be inherited.

Evidence of the lifestyle of *H. floresiensis* includes small stone tools and blades similar to those used by other *Homo* species for scraping and butchering meat, and the remains of charred bones. This evidence suggests that this species was adept at hunting and cooking meat over a fire.

It is the timing of *H. floresiensis* that troubles some paleoanthropologists. It has been suggested that the species lived on Flores until about 12,000 years ago, when a massive volcanic eruption could have wiped them out. Having lived until 12,000 years ago would make them the most recently extinct example of *Homo* that was not anatomically modern. *H. floresiensis* continued to flourish in relative isolation, it seems, for about 18,000 years after the last of the Neandertals.

The reason for the dwarfism of *H. floresiensis* probably is related to their island habitat. Although *H. floresiensis* has a body size comparable to that of australopithecines, *H. floresiensis's* other derived features—face, teeth, jaws, and posture—also link it to more derived *Homo* species. It would appear that a group of members of an early *Homo* species—possibly *H. erectus*—became isolated on this island and adapted dwarfism in response to environmental conditions of this habitat, one of which may have been reduced energy requirements that favored small body size. The so-called island effect has been observed in animals other than hominins. Flores itself includes dwarf species of other animals, including a form of elephant.

Thus far, the evolutionary links between *H. floresiensis* and other hominins are still being worked out. The evolutionary connections of human ancestry certainly are made more complicated when it appears that a species such as *H. floresiensis* could have forged its own unique trail for so long in such isolation from other species.

Some of the ambiguities of *Homo* evolution relate to the time of known species' appearance and their geographic location. *H. floresiensis* is a surprise in this regard, having had no fossil history from older hominin settlements in Africa, Europe, and Asia. One must believe that we are in for even more surprises as fieldwork continues in other isolated places on the globe.

BECOMING MODERN *HOMO*

Ian Tattersall remarks that the most important evolutionary developments leading to modern humans were the advent of "uprightness, toolmaking, and striding bipedalism." Uprightness changed our anatomy from that of forest dwellers to occupiers of open spaces. Toolmaking represented the ability of hominins to improve their lifestyle by changing the odds and devising strategies for survival that involved tools for hunting and preparing food. "Striding bipedalism" made humans mobile, allowing them to migrate beyond their homelands and spread their kind from Africa to Europe, western Asia, and beyond in a matter of tens of thousands of years.

The fossil record of pre–*H. sapiens* hominins also shows that there was more than one path to longevity. *H. heidelbergensis, H. neanderthalensis,* and *H. floresiensis* all were successful species of *Homo* that thrived for a long time despite dramatic changes to their world—both geographically and climatically—and in the face of threats from predators that ranged from big cats to viruses and diseases. They survived for hundreds of thousands of years.

Chapter 4 explores the rise of modern humans as the best example yet of hominin adaptability.

SUMMARY

This chapter examined the most recent *Homo* species to emerge during the past 500,000 years, just prior to and alongside the rise of modern humans in the form of *Homo sapiens*.

1. The Pleistocene Epoch is also called the Ice Age because during this time, large glacial masses advanced and retreated periodically in cycles that lasted about 100,000 years.

2. Glacial periods had two consequences for the migration patterns of humans and other mammals. Migration from Africa to Europe was blocked by extensive deserts of northern Africa. As glaciers advanced in the Northern Hemisphere, land bridges formed that permitted the migration of humans and other animals to adjoining landmasses, such as a link between Asia and North America.

3. The species *Homo heidelbergensis* includes several widespread hominin specimens found throughout the Old World. They had a more modern skull and larger brain capacity than *H. erectus*. *H. heidelbergensis* spans a time frame from about 200,000 to 525,000 years ago.

4. *Homo neanderthalensis*, the Neandertals, are a species of *Homo* that arose in Europe about 200,000 years ago, became widespread throughout Europe and western Asia by about 120,000 years ago, and became extinct only 25,000 years ago.

5. Fossil evidence and a comparison of the *H. neanderthalensis* and *H. sapiens* genomes confirm that Neandertals were a *Homo* species separate from all others.

6. Neandertals were masters of the Levallois and Mousterian toolmaking technologies.

7. Neandertals were hunters. They lived in caves, rock shelters, and outside shelters that they made, and they buried their dead. Although anatomically and genetically capable of using verbal language, it is unknown whether Neandertals had a spoken language.

8. *Homo floresiensis* is a recently discovered *Homo* species from the island of Flores in Indonesia. It was a dwarf species of *Homo* with a combination of archaic and modern anatomical traits. Having lived until 12,000 years ago, *H. floresiensis* was the last *Homo* of the nonanatomically modern *Homo* species to become extinct.

4

The Emergence of Modern Humans—*Homo sapiens*

It is impossible not to admire the Neandertals. For the better part of the past 200,000 years, this unique group of early humans represented the best and most advanced version of what hominins had to offer. They suffered through a progression of unspeakable trials. Geologically, Neandertals adjusted to a planet that changed, cruelly, from moderately comfortable to extremely cold for thousands of years at a time and to migration paths that opened and closed with changing glacial conditions. They were threatened continually by the presence of large, predatory creatures that included cave bears, big cats, and giant hyenas. Yet Neandertals persisted and thrived, relying on their intelligence and adaptability to radiate throughout the glacial regions of Europe and western Asia.

Neandertals had a stick-to-itiveness that cannot be denied. What they apparently lacked in symbolic thinking and thoughtfulness, they apparently made up for by their great strength and resolve. Neandertals were largely an unchanging lot. Once they solved a problem, they seem to have stuck with the same solution, generation after generation. Their tools were an elaboration of those of earlier Stone Age artisans but did not advance beyond the admittedly difficult-to-master Levallois technology for flaking one rock with another.

Neandertals' spears and other weapons were designed for close combat and never advanced to the kinds of long-distance and stealth weapons used by later humans, such as spear-throwing devices, slings, and the bow and arrow. Neandertals stuck with what worked for them and rarely veered from the path that had brought them past success.

About 40,000 years ago, Neandertals apparently encountered an obstacle for which they were not well prepared. It was at about that time the earliest modern peoples—*Homo sapiens*—invaded the turf of *H. neanderthalensis*. Within 10,000 years of this first encounter, Neandertals were extinct, apparently unable to compete for resources with a growing population of anatomically modern humans whose language, more effective weapons, mobility, and community culture made them overwhelmingly superior opponents.

This chapter explores the emergence of *Homo sapiens*, their biology, their geographic radiation, and the aspects of their early culture that laid the foundation for their longevity as the only surviving species of the *Homo* taxon today.

DEFINING *HOMO SAPIENS*

The term anatomically modern human refers to the species *Homo sapiens*, the only living species of hominin. Features that distinguish *H. sapiens* from other hominins include a flatter, smaller face whose jaw does not jut out; no heavy, joined brow ridges; a rounded rather than elongated cranial shape; a vertical rather than sloping forehead; and a protruding chin. The human brain capacity averages 1,350 cc, and the top of the skull lacks the bony crest for the attachment of large neck and jaw muscles that is seen in earlier hominins. The human eye sockets are smaller; the teeth are smaller, especially in the front; and the skeleton is generally taller, less robust, and less muscular than in ancestral hominins.

It is widely accepted that the earliest hominins originated in Africa, but the origin of the species *H. sapiens* has been more controversial. There are proponents of an African origin as well as proponents of origins in Asia.

Two lines of evidence support an African origin for *H. sapiens*. The first line is the fossil record, wherein three hominin skulls with fully modern appearance have been found in deposits in Ethiopia that date from 160,000 years ago. A second line of evidence for

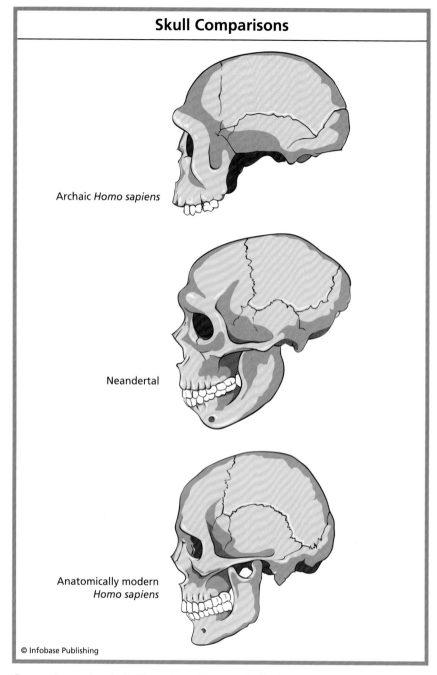

Skull Comparisons

Archaic *Homo sapiens*

Neandertal

Anatomically modern
Homo sapiens

Comparison of archaic *H. sapiens*, *H. neanderthalensis*, and modern
H. sapiens

an African origin comes from the study of human DNA. Comparisons of modern human DNA taken from people whose ancestors populated all of the major continents provide clues to the historical stages of human genetic makeup. This research shows that mitochondrial DNA—DNA contained in the cytoplasm of a cell—from African populations contains greater variation than does DNA from populations in other locations. The implication is that *H. sapiens* has existed in Africa longer than the species has existed on any other continent. This proposition has been called the Mitochondrial Eve Theory. The theory was first proposed in 1987 by a team of biochemists including Rebecca L. Cann, Mark Stoneking, and Allan C. Wilson. The researchers calculated that the **gene pool** comprising modern humans first came into being about 170,000 years ago—a conclusion that does not conflict with the oldest known fossils of modern humans.

Not everyone agrees with the statistical methods employed to calculate these results. Milford Wolpoff points out that the central observation of the Eve Theory "is the fact that genetic variation within populations is much greater than between populations." While this conclusion could mean that human populations have a "recent common origin," it also could mean that different populations had been exchanging genes for a long time, and that variations from each population have been combined. Paleoanthropologist John Relethford has shown that the increased variation attributed to DNA of African origin also might be due to the large size of ancient African populations and variation that occurred within this large population. The controversies surrounding the origins of *H. sapiens* are explored further later in the chapter, in "Origins and Radiation of Modern Humans."

Slightly more recent fossils than those from Ethiopia show that *H. sapiens* first spread to the Near East, where fossils of modern humans dating from 120,000 years ago have been found in Israel. Fossils also appear in China by about 50,000 years ago as well as in Australia about the same time. Interestingly, *H. sapiens* is not known from western Europe until about 40,000 years ago, when specimens known as Cro-Magnon—after a French fossil site—begin to show up. *H. sapiens* apparently first spread from Africa to the Near and Far East before invading the glacial homelands of the Neandertals in Europe.

EARLY *HOMO SAPIENS* SPECIMENS FROM AFRICA AND THE NEAR EAST

Arranged from oldest to youngest specimens

Location	Time (years ago)	Description
Ethiopia (Herto)	154,000 to 160,000	Skull and jaw fragments of 4 individuals
South Africa (Klasies River mouth)	84,000 to 120,000	Fragmentary, several individuals
Israel (Qafzeh)	92,000 to 120,000	20 individuals
Israel (Skhül)	81,000 to 101,000	10 individuals

Following the rise of early or archaic *H. sapiens* in Africa and the Near East, there was a great dispersal of this new species across the Old World. Just how this took place is the subject of the section "Origins and Radiation of Modern Humans." By about 30,000 years ago, *H. sapiens* are found in such distant places as Australia and China. Their move into western Europe, between 30,000 and 40,000 years ago, overlapped with the presence of Neandertals. It is supposed that similar convergences of archaic *Homo* species occurred in other parts of the world, where *H. erectus* was still present but on the wane as a species.

Many gaps remain in the fossil record of early *H. sapiens*. In Asia, little is known about the presence of anatomically modern humans from about 40,000 to 100,000 years ago. The fact that *H. sapiens* remains that date from about 50,000 years ago have been found in Australia indicates that modern humans of at least the same approximate age were present in Asia, a stepping-off point for accessing the Indonesian islands and Australia.

EARLY *HOMO SAPIENS* SPECIMENS FROM EUROPE, ASIA, AND AUSTRALIA

Arranged from oldest to youngest specimens

Location	Time (years ago)	Description
Australia (Lake Mungo)	40,000	3 individuals
France (Cro-Magnon)	30,000	8 individuals
Czech Republic (Predmostí)	26,000	29 individuals
Portugal (Abrigo do Lagar Velho)	24,500	1 individual (child)
China (Zhoukoudian)	10,000 to 18,000	8 individuals
Australia (Kow Swamp)	9,000 to 14,000	40 individuals (many ages)

ORIGINS AND RADIATION OF MODERN HUMANS

A simplified view of the evolution of modern humans assumes the emergence of the species *H. sapiens* from an ancestral line of ever-more-derived hominins for which brain size and bipedalism were paramount to these hominins' adaptive success. Choosing an ancestor for anatomically modern humans is more complicated than simply comparing the anatomical traits of ancestral candidates, however. The matter of the early geographic dispersal of *Homo* species to the far reaches of the Old World greatly complicates the issue of determining when and where the first *H. sapiens* actually emerged. It is a discussion full of puzzles. Why do *H. sapiens* appear in Australia at about the same time or even earlier than they do in Europe? Did the species actually develop in Asia first and then work its way back to Europe? Or, did *H. sapiens* arise in more than one location along independently developing branches of the *H. erectus* lineage?

The incompleteness of the fossil record is the chief obstacle to solving this mystery. Paleoanthropologists work with the best available information to ascertain the sequence of evolutionary events leading to the advent of modern humans. Because, however, it is difficult to complete a jigsaw puzzle when most of the pieces are missing, there remain several respectable hypotheses about the emergence and distribution of *H. sapiens.* Two convincing models of *H. sapiens* evolution currently are in play, and each has its variations. These models are the Replacement Model (also known as the Recent African Origin Model) and the Regional Continuity Model (also known as the Multiregional Origins Model).

The Replacement Model of *H. Sapiens* Evolution

The emergence of *H. sapiens* is easier to picture when it is viewed as an "Out of Africa" scenario. According to this scenario, *H. sapiens* evolved in Africa about 200,000 years ago, radiated out of this area throughout the Old World, and replaced all separate species of *Homo* that lived in those places, including Neandertals. This model was proposed in 1988 by British paleoanthropologists Christopher Stringer and Peter Andrews.

The Replacement Model is sometimes called the Recent African Origin Model because it depends on the hypothesis that *H. sapiens* is a relatively recent species that arose from ancestral lineages of Africa. This model does not recognize any transitional hominin forms bridging the gap from archaic to anatomically modern humans except for those found in Africa. In its strictest definition, this model presumes that *H. sapiens* emerged from Africa as a completely separate species, and that there was no interbreeding of *H. sapiens* with other hominin populations that had taken root outside of Africa. *H. sapiens* simply outcompeted other local hominin populations in Europe and Asia, utterly replacing them.

In 2002, Stringer himself modified his view to accept the possibility of limited interbreeding between *H. sapiens* and premodern forms such as *H. heidelbergensis* and *H. neanderthalensis.* By accepting some interbreeding as part of the model, researchers acknowledge that archaic humans would have contributed to the gene pool of modern humans—a fact that explains some variations seen in a range of *H. sapiens* specimens from eastern Europe, Asia, and other regions. From the standpoint of the lumper and splitter points of view discussed in Chapter 2, the acceptance of possible interbreeding between *H. sapiens* and archaic humans moves the Replacement Model away from a splitter point of view in the direction of the lumper standpoint. That standpoint is also the basis for the Regional Continuity Model described below. The lessons here are that in science, there is room for disagreement, compromise, and the correction of error, and that the lines between different hypotheses are not always as clearly drawn as they might appear to the nonscientist.

Several lines of evidence continue to support the Replacement Model. The earliest fossil hominins, including anatomically modern humans, are found in Africa. When the dates of these fossils are compared with the dates of hominin fossils found outside Africa, there is a definite impression that humans radiated out of Africa to Europe, the Near East, Asia, and Indonesia. By about 18,000 years ago, the only human species that remained, with the exception of *H. floresiensis*, was *H. sapiens*. There are, however, clearly fossils of modern humans—from Portugal and the Czech Republic in particular—that exhibit a mosaic of traits seemingly like those of Neandertals and modern humans. Furthermore, as paleoanthropologist Augustin Fuentes of the University of Notre Dame points out, several populations of modern humans around the world exhibit such so-called archaic traits as brow ridges, large teeth, and robust lower jaws. These examples strongly suggest that the Replacement Model must accept some degree of interbreeding between early *H. sapiens* and other premodern *Homo* populations.

Evidence from genetic studies, including the Eve Theory discussed earlier, also supports the Replacement Model. This suggests that the first major split in the lineage of *H. sapiens* was between Africans and non-Africans, and that this speciation first occurred about 200,000 years ago.

The Regional Continuity Model of *H. sapiens* Evolution

The story of human evolution contains some complexities that the Replacement Model cannot easily explain. To some paleoanthropologists, the human species has been intact for longer than

200,000 years, and variations seen in the fossil record are not indicative of the existence of separate species that would have been incapable of interbreeding. The Regional Continuity Model, proposed by Milford Wolpoff and his colleagues in 1994, takes into consideration aspects of the fossil record that are not easily resolved by the Replacement Model. The Regional Continuity Model says that modern human populations evolved simultaneously on their respective continents following the initial radiation of archaic humans out of Africa.

The Regional Continuity Model, sometimes called the Multiregional Model, first denies the existence of separate *Homo* species that could not have interbred. In doing this, it takes a lumpers point of view in respect to *H. sapiens* evolution. Lumpers consider all archaic *Homo* species as part of one large population capable of interbreeding. According to this model, *Homo* spread throughout Africa, Europe, and Asia, and modern humans evolved simultaneously in different regions from existing local populations. This process assumes that individual populations of *Homo* underwent similar kinds of changes in different parts of the world. The interbreeding of individuals from different populations over a long period of time resulted in shared genes that now are found in *H. sapiens*. The Regional Continuity Model accounts for deeply rooted variations seen today in populations from different parts of the world and assumes that premodern humans contributed to the gene pool that eventually formed the basis of *H. sapiens*.

While at first this theory appears to suggest the unlikely possibility that the species *H. sapiens* evolved simultaneously in different locations, this would not actually have been the case because no population was entirely isolated from the others. Through geographic migration, various populations of early humans would have met, interbred, and created a shared gene pool that now forms the basis of the species. Proponents of the Regional Continuity Model suggest that such contact between humans from different regions would have been enough to maintain the single species *H. sapiens*.

Two Models of Human Origins

Recent African Origin

Europe   Africa   Asia

Modern *Homo sapiens*

Archaic species of
Homo, now extinct

Regional Continuity Model

Europe   Africa   Asia

Homo sapiens

Gene flow

Note: Based on Fuentes
© Infobase Publishing

Two models of human origins

Another interesting approach to understanding the origin and radiation of modern humans is to compare the genetic makeup of **extant** peoples of the world. Based on studies of DNA, scientists have been able to trace the possible migration routes of early peoples. When such genetic data are combined with paleoclimate data and fossil records of human remains, an intriguing scenario is formed that fits most neatly with the "Out of Africa" hypotheses of modern human origins. According to these data, the first radiation of modern humans came out of East Africa about 100,000 years ago and moved into other parts of Africa and Asia. Two routes were taken into Asia. The earlier of these routes hugged the coast of southern and southeastern Asia and then divided, with one path going south and another heading north into China, Japan, and eventually on to the **New World** by land bridge. The second Asian route was northerly. It took early humans into the Middle East and Central Asia, at which point it radiated in all directions, including westward to Europe and eastward toward the New World. This pattern of radiation is illustrated in the accompanying map.

Although this DNA-based radiation pattern superficially supports the Replacement Model of *H. sapiens* dispersal, to some extent, it also suggests the widespread interaction and interbreeding of *Homo* species, possibly archaic with modern, in the various regions to and from which these peoples migrated.

THE CULTURE OF EARLY *HOMO SAPIENS*

Throughout *The Prehistoric Earth*, the geologic time scale has been used consistently to date the times during which any given species existed. This system works well when time frames are being measured in the millions and hundreds of thousands of years. As the discussion of human evolution of the Pleistocene Epoch edges closer to the current epoch in which we live—the Holocene— paleoanthropologists have found it to be convenient to use an alternative time scale for marking significant stages in the development of humans and their culture. Instead of using geologically based terms such as *Pleistocene* (for the most recent glacial age) and

Holocene (the time of our present climate), they have adopted the term *Paleolithic* ("old stone age"), a term that is based on the evolutionary development of human anatomy and culture.

Lower Paleolithic (250,000 to 500,000 years ago). The time of archaic hominins.

Middle Paleolithic (60,000 to 250,000 years ago). The time of Neandertals and premodern *Homo*.

Upper Paleolithic (Europe, 10,000 to 60,000 years ago). The time of anatomically modern *Homo*.

The time of the emergence of modern *H. sapiens* in Europe is the Upper Paleolithic. This span of human prehistory overlaps the geologic time scale at approximately 11,550 years ago, marking the end of the Pleistocene and the most recent Ice Age. Even before the end of the Ice Age, however, the revolution stirred by the rise of *H. sapiens* was beginning to expand exponentially and to touch most geographic regions of the planet. Modern humans were highly mobile. They adapted quickly to a variety of environmental conditions and quickly forged strong cultural traditions that could be taught to others and passed along from one generation to the next. Even glaciers and continental ice sheets could not prevent their rapid radiation.

The artifacts associated with modern humans appear during the Upper Paleolithic, beginning at about 50,000 years ago in Europe (earlier in Africa). This development appeared to be the evolutionary payoff for having developed large brains and bipedalism: Humans began to challenge their environment, adapt to a wider range of habitats, and change their behaviors as never before. The result is a rich archaeological record that provides many clues to the culture of early modern humans.

H. sapiens Technology

The Upper Paleolithic tool technology of *H. sapiens* was more sophisticated in several ways than the Mousterian toolmaking methods of Neandertals. Even thought the Neandertals had succeeded in developing a wide variety of specialized flake tools, the variety of tools and the methods of making them did not change much in their culture. *H. sapiens* toolmaking also was stone based, but it began to systematically include the use of stone in combination with other materials, such as bone, antlers, and wood. Most importantly, *H. sapiens'* new technology included **blade tools**, each crafted from a stone flake that was twice as long as it was wide. The blade added a new dimension to the repertoire of flake tools and greatly extended the tool kit of early humans.

Blade tools of varying degrees of thickness and sharpness were used as burins for shaping wood and bone; as borers for punching holes in skins, bones and other materials; and as scraping knives with smooth or serrated edges. Blade tools were more complicated to make than Mousterian tools. Producing blade tools required additional planning and practice, such as finding an appropriate stone core, fashioning a striking platform from which to cut blades, and using one or more techniques to strike a flake from the core. Prepared core technology is a key feature of Upper Paleolithic toolmaking.

Anthropologist Conrad Kottak explains that the Upper Paleolithic process for making blades was faster and less wasteful than Mousterian technology: The Upper Paleolithic process produced 15 times the amount of cutting edge from the same amount of core material. It is also evident that between 17,000 and 40,000 years ago, *H. sapiens* not only increased the number of tool types available, but also began to manufacture them in a standardized manner that increased the production of quality tools.

H. sapiens were more effective than Neandertals at reconceptualizing tools. *H. sapiens* found ways to combine different kinds of objects for new purposes. It was during the Upper Paleolithic that stone blades were hafted—tied—to wooden shafts to produce throwing spears. One of the most effective hunting weapons of the time was the atlatl, or spear-thrower, examples of which have been found in Upper Paleolithic remains of western Europe. The atlatl consists of a piece of wood about a foot long with a handle at one end and a hooked pocket on the back to hold the blunt end of a spear or dart. Using an atlatl increased the accuracy and distance of the throw and provided a deadly weapon that could be used from a safer distance than normal, unassisted spear throwing. A few early examples of spear-throwers have been found in remains that date from the Middle Paleolithic, but spear-throwers from the Upper Paleolithic were the first to include elaborately sculpted or engraved images on the handle. The atlatl was widely used by Upper Paleolithic peoples but soon was supplanted by the even more deadly bow and arrow, the first examples of which begin to appear during the Upper Paleolithic.

Along with advancing technology for launching projectiles came many varieties of deadly points made of wood, stone, bone, and antler. The sharpest of these probably were designed to pierce the hide of particular kinds of animals. The barbed and sawlike varieties most likely were used to spear fish. Darts may have been used to hunt birds.

New technologies improved humans' access to food and allowed them to add new sources of nutrition to their diet. The most obvious evidence of Upper Paleolithic food still consists of the bones of large animals and the tools used to kill, butcher, and prepare meat for consumption, but there also exists less obvious evidence for the increased sophistication of humans' plant consumption. Traces of seeds, nutshells, and pollen found at many fossil sites attest to a diet rich in berries, nuts, and other vegetation. Clifford Jolly points out that close examination of cutting tools has revealed evidence for the chopping and slicing of various grasses that might have been a part of the diet of early humans.

In 1981, Canadian paleoanthropologist Brian Hayden of Simon Fraser University hypothesized that the change from a glacial to more temperate worldwide climate dramatically changed the nature of human subsistence patterns. With the retreat of glacial ice sheets by about 10,000 years ago, world climates also changed in ways that benefited expanding human populations. Temperatures rose, and patterns of precipitation transformed landscapes. While conditions during the Pleistocene were dry, the Holocene Epoch that followed was more humid, and that humidity spurred increased plant growth.

Once-arid grasslands above the equator became dense woodlands. Below the equator, in Africa, grasslands were transformed into tropical rain forests.

Animals that once were adapted to glacial climates found it difficult to survive in the new hot and wet climates. The demise of such cold-adapted creatures as the woolly mammoths created opportunities, however, for other creatures that were better adapted for forests. Humans once again showed their remarkable talent for using intelligence and technology to change with the changing world around them. They found ways to cultivate new plants and devised different weapons and strategies for hunting wild game.

The *H. sapiens* culture of the Upper Paleolithic often is characterized as a hunter-gatherer society. Hunter-gatherers are people who depend on natural resources for their subsistence. They live off of the plants and animals available around them and do not cultivate vegetation or livestock. By the end of the Upper Paleolithic, however, changing climate conditions and growing populations put a strain on traditional hunter-gatherer lifestyles. Hayden suggests that more favorable climate conditions led to an intensification of the use of resources such as food and shelter and to the development of an increasingly diverse array of technologies to cope with the provisioning of resources. Simply put, societies were becoming larger; were using up the local plant and animal resources more quickly; and, because of their size, were less able to pick up and move to exploit natural resources elsewhere. These trends represent the advent of Mesolithic economies, the next stage of human cultures of the Middle Paleolithic. One result of this was an adaptation to food resources that could be replenished more quickly than previous resources. Jolly suggests a shift from hunting for the largest, less populous game, such as mammoths, to hunting for more plentiful animals that also reproduced quickly, such as rabbits, deer, fish, and shellfish. This adaptation also included a shift toward plentiful plants foods such as grains and nuts.

A refinement of this intensification of resource use eventually led to the domestication of animals and crops, a practice that began between 8,000 and 10,000 years ago in the Near East and subsequently appeared in Europe and the New World between 4,000 and 7,000 years ago.

Settlements and Shelters

Whereas evidence of Middle Paleolithic shelters associated with Neandertals is restricted mostly to caves and rock shelters, there appears to have been a veritable housing boom among *H. sapiens* of the Upper Paleolithic. While caves and rock shelters remained popular, there is much evidence for human-built shelters in open spaces, often miles from the nearest cave formations. What remains are the animal bones that once were used to hold down the edges of animal skins that probably were stretched over a wooden frame. Some shelters had floors consisting of smooth river stones. When living in caves, *H. sapiens* often divided the shelter into areas devoted to specific activities, such as butchering, cooking, garbage disposal, and sleeping. In short, modern humans were a better-organized bunch than Neandertals.

Picking the best location for a settlement was also apparently on the minds of Upper Paleolithic peoples. In Europe, most evidence of rock-shelter dwellings indicates that *H. sapiens* preferred a southern exposure to provide a form of natural thermal regulation with the rising and falling of the sun. Several studies also have shown that social groups sometimes moved with the seasons and selected their sites to maximize access to plant or animal food resources. Choosing a site that was near a known seasonal migration path for a prey animal such as reindeer made it much easier to hunt these animals.

Upper Paleolithic groups appear to have been mobile, staying on the move throughout the year to follow the availability of plant and animal resources. As hunter-gatherers, they did not remain permanently in any location, and they probably moved about in small groups for most of the year. Depending on the region, there may have been times when large groups gathered in one location to exploit a seasonal resource such as a migratory herd of animals or a seasonal plant food. Based on evidence of shelters from the fossil record, individual huts sometimes were large enough to house as many as 25 people, perhaps the outer size limit of a natural family unit. The Lower Paleolithic site at Terra Amata (see Chapter 2) is interpreted by some paleoanthropologists as a site to which humans returned seasonally for hunting purposes.

Gathering seasonally into large groups would have created new social opportunities for early peoples. These occasions might have been a time for exchanging goods with others and for strengthening the social bonds between otherwise independent groups of hunter-gatherers. These meetings could be viewed as another important stage in the gradual evolution of human social culture leading to practices that eventually flowered in the establishment of permanent communities and basic rules of social engagement.

Language

The evolution of the larger brain of *Homo,* coupled with that brain's division into hemispheres, maximized the storage and cognitive capacity of modern humans. This added capacity for processing information was accompanied by the gradual development of a verbal communication system that is unique to humans. The evolution of human language and of the cognitive skills required by language give people a means to store, convey, recreate, and pass along cultural information that is critical to society. Imagine how limited human culture would be without the ability to store information using symbolic language: The substance of culture would be limited by what could be acted out with the body or possessed as an object in the material world. Language, on the other hand, exponentially expands the ability of a society to create, preserve, and convey the ideas, experiences, and lessons that enable the human species to remain viable.

Apes have the innate ability to remember and use verbal expressions. Several historically important studies have shown that apes can be taught to communicate with humans through the use of such techniques as American Sign Language or through images shown on a computer screen. In 1966, the husband and wife team of Beatrix T. Gardner (1933–2008) and R. Allen Gardner demonstrated that a young chimp could be taught to communicate using American Sign Language. This pioneering work led to many follow-up studies using a variety of communication methods.

When it comes to language capability, what apes lack and humans possess is a talent for recombining such linguistic elements into entirely new combinations and meanings. Language requires several components: a lexicon of words (the vocabulary) and rules for combining those words into structured sentences. The rules of grammar and sentence structure are called syntax. The individual sounds that make up words are called phonemes, and the words themselves—meaningful combinations of phonemes—are known as morphemes. Apes not only lack the ability to combine phonemes into an infinite number of morphemes, but also lack the cognitive ability to work with a lexicon of rules in their thoughts. Therein lies the difference between the verbal calls of a chimpanzee and the poetry of a human.

It is presumed that Upper Paleolithic humans used spoken language. The use of spoken language is one of the reasons given for humans' meteoric rise to the top of the *Homo* heap at the likely expense of other hominin species around them. One aspect of early *H. sapiens* success was the development of a strong social network of smaller groups. Research in the development of language shows that language is linked to the social success of the human species. Wolpoff points out several social functions of language that seem to have been in play among *H. sapiens* of the Upper Paleolithic:

- Language represents complex social relations that are based on mutual expectations.
- Language creates social systems and forges alliances between people.

- Language encourages the naming and identification of individuals.
- Language permits strategic planning.
- Language stimulates differences between groups that might require action. Such action—such as a disagreement over traded goods—might be communicated or reinforced using art or symbols.

Written language did not evolve until about 5,300 years ago, in Sumer, a country between the Tigris and Euphrates rivers in present-day Iraq. In the approximately 5,000 years between the Upper Paleolithic and the Sumerian civilization, *H. sapiens* practiced the use of verbal language as well as symbolic expression in their art and handicrafts.

Burials

In contrast to Neandertals, for whom burial might have been no more than an exercise in the removal of carcasses, modern humans began to practice burials as a more symbolic act. Evidence of *H. sapiens* burials begins to appear in the fossil record by about 28,000 years ago. The nature of the grave sites varies from region to region, but most grave sites involve burial pits and often contain "grave goods," objects interpreted as symbolic ornamentation that were placed intentionally on the body when it was buried. Jolly points out that one-third of known Upper Paleolithic burial sites include two or more individuals buried together.

The configuration and treatment of bodies also varies greatly. Whereas Neandertal graves almost always contain bodies that have been somewhat bent, the bodies of Upper Paleolithic humans have been found in graves in a variety of configurations, from fully doubled over to moderately bent to lying straight.

Ritual treatment of corpses may range from the provision of different amounts and kinds of grave goods with a body to various ways in which the body was dismembered or colored with natural pigments. The attention given to a grave might have been a reflection of the social standing of an individual. In one most unusual case, in the Czech Republic, paleoanthropologist Bohuslav Klima of the Czech Academy of Sciences described the circumstances of three individuals buried alongside one another. The triple burial was uncovered in 1987 in the town of Dolni Vestonice. The body in the middle was that of a teenage female who suffered from such deformities as a shortened leg, a deformed face, and a crippled arm. She was flanked by two males of about the same age. The male to her right had a wooden stake driven through his pelvis, and his right hand was outstretched to cover the woman's pelvic area. The male to the woman's left was lying face down, with his head turned away from the woman and his left arm on top of her left arm. The males each had beads on their heads, and the pelvic region of the female had been stained red with ochre pigment. The face of one male had also been painted in a masklike manner.

While the exact circumstances leading up to this highly symbolic burial cannot be known for sure, Klima believes that the individuals were all buried at the same time and that the special treatment given their bodies may have reflected some distinctive social connection. Were the three related? Did the woman die while giving birth? Were the men somehow implicated in her fate? Was this a form of ritualized justice?

The Dolni Vestonice story is one of the more unusual ones involving Upper Paleolithic burials, but it is not the only one that involves the special treatment of individuals in a manner that might be considered especially symbolic and meaningful. In 1995, science author James Shreeve considered Klima's account and interpreted the burial as a possible example of ritual sacrifice. "The two male skeletons were those of her husband and a medicine man—the man wearing the mask," wrote Shreeve. "Held responsible for her death, the men had been compelled to follow her into the afterlife."

Italian paleoanthropologist Vincenzo Formicola of the University of Pisa has conducted several studies of multiple graves sites in Upper Paleolithic Europe. In 2007, he published a report on three of the most peculiar: the Dolni Vestonice site in the Czech Republic, a double burial of a preteen boy and girl in Russia, and the burial of a teenage dwarf boy in the arms of an adult female in Russia. In all three cases, young individuals were involved, one individual in the grave had a physical deformity, and unusual grave goods were present. In each case, it appears that healthy individuals may have gone to the grave with an infirm person who died. Formicola suspects that these all were cases of ritual sacrifice, a practice that has not been widely considered for the Upper Paleolithic fossil record.

Arts

Unlike their Neandertal contemporaries, modern humans dedicated much time and energy to the production of symbolic objects and art. Much of this work is remarkable in its depictions of animals, people, and aspects of life in the Upper Paleolithic. Objects of art found in such early societies often had both functional and aesthetic qualities. Stone tools and weapons sometimes were adorned with engravings of animals or geometric patterns. The decoration of practical objects such as tools suggests that an innate appreciation of design and decoration is part of human nature. The impulse to create works of artistic interest and beauty appears to be part of the genome of *H. sapiens*.

The fossil record of Upper Paleolithic peoples includes objects made for personal ornamentation or as hand-held sculpture that go back about 30,000 years. Items such as small carved figures of people and animals have been found throughout Europe and Asia. Some are carved from bone, ivory, wood, or stone; others are shaped from clay. The skill and imagination required to create such works are fully modern. One example, found in Germany, is a remarkable carving, about 12 inches (30 cm) tall, that was made between 26,000 and 30,000 years ago. Sculpted from a piece of mammoth tusk, it depicts an upright figure that resembles a man but with a lion's head and **forelimbs** instead of a human head and arms. Art historian Marilyn Stokstad notes that this sculpture clearly is a work from the imagination rather than a copy from nature. Thus, even at this early stage in the development of art, humans already had become engaged in a thinking process that transcended the mere imitation of reality—an enduring, underlying theme and motivation even for the most forward-looking art of our own time. Other examples of small animal sculptures in many styles are found throughout Europe and Asia.

Female figures are the most common form of human sculpture found from the Upper Paleolithic. The styles and the materials used to create these sculptures vary widely. The Woman of Willendorf is a small stone sculpture, 24,000 years old, from Austria. The Willendorf artist greatly exaggerated the rounded form of the woman's head, breasts, torso (the figure is possibly pregnant), and legs. The figure most likely was created as a depiction of female fertility and good fortune. Other female figures are less exaggerated, such as a small female figurine discovered in the Czech Republic and known as the Woman from Ostrava Petrkovice. She was carved 23,000 years ago. The partial figure is made of the mineral hematite. The woman is a more slender, fit individual than the Woman of Willendorf and is depicted in a pose that suggests walking.

Beads, pendants, and other forms of personal ornamentation made from bone, ivory, stone, and clay also were common. The making of female fertility figures and other likenesses of people and animals suggests to many anthropologists that art played a role in the lives of early peoples as a means of acting out symbolic behavior, possibly as part of rituals that were part of local cultures.

Another form of art for which Upper Paleolithic peoples are known is cave painting. More than 350 sites of cave art are known, primarily in France and Spain. Only 150 years ago, most of these sites still were unknown. This is primarily because such paintings often are located in caves that are hidden or difficult to access. While the caves frequently show evidence that groups of humans sometimes occupied them, it appears that the caves often were too remote and inaccessible to have served as permanent shelters. Instead, the caves served as gathering places for special purposes. There is evidence that some caves were visited over the course of hundreds of years. The purpose of the cave paintings, it seems, possibly was related to rituals for which the group occasionally would gather.

The earliest cave art dates from 32,000 years ago and is found at Chauvet, in France. The caves of Lascaux, in Dordogne, France, are much younger; they date from about 15,000 to 17,000 years ago. Lascaux is well known for its large number of images and remarkably colorful depictions of painted animals. Of the nearly 2,000 wall paintings found in Lascaux, many depict horses, bison, and deer. A smaller number provide glimpses of birds, cats, bears, a rhinoceros, and at least one person. The Altimira cave in Spain dates from about the same time as Lascaux and is known for its actual tools and other objects as well as for wall and ceiling paintings of animals and human hands. Cave paintings found in Africa, Southeast Asia, and Australia are decidedly younger, dating from about 2,000 years ago.

Some caves include evidence for the materials and methods used to create these paintings. Paints were applied using fingers or brushes made of hair or by a blowing technique in which the artist sprayed color pigment from the mouth, using the hand or other objects to stencil broad shapes on the cave wall. The color pigments used came from naturally occurring materials such as iron oxide—red ochre—and charcoal. Stone lamps filled with animal fat would have been used to light a dark interior so that an artist could work.

It once was thought that cave paintings of animals were created to provide good fortune on the hunt. Studies by French anthropologists André Leroi-Gourhan (1911–1986) and Annette Laming (1917–1977) showed, however, that this probably was not the case because the animals most often depicted in the caves were not the ones most frequently consumed by the clan. Furthermore, the two researchers each detected consistent patterns for the spatial organization of specific animal images in many of the caves that they studied. The making of cave art apparently was a thoughtful, well-planned activity that may have been preconceived with other rituals and group activities in mind.

A Lascaux cave painting

INTO THE MODERN

The foundations of human culture evolved rapidly after the establishment of anatomically modern humans. The earliest human records from the Upper Paleolithic include refined works of sculptural and painted art. Humans' tool technology became diverse in the perfection of specialized devices for many practical purposes and began to integrate materials other than stone. The development of human thought—the conceptual mind—is also evident in the planning, imagination, and functions illustrated by many kinds of fossil evidence: the optimal locations of dwellings; the spatial organization of early human homes; the planning of ritual spaces, such as caves, where wall paintings provided the context for social gatherings; the making of blade tools; burials that hint at sacrifice and ritual; and strategies for effectively hunting, butchering, cooking, and sharing animal food. It is most likely that language also was one of the attributes that began to flower during these early stages in the rise of *H. sapiens.*

The close of the Upper Paleolithic brought the world's hunter-gatherer tribes to the threshold of a new stage in the evolution of humans and their culture. As recently as 20,000 years ago, humans still lived in relatively small, mobile groups that lived off the land. Increasing population sizes required new strategies for provisioning food, leading to the first domestication of plants and animals. As settlements became larger, people's mobility lessened. By about 5,000 years ago, large population centers had emerged, and the era of documented history commenced with the advent of writing.

The intervening years from the Upper Paleolithic to the present saw an explosion of additional technological, social, and cultural changes in the human race. Humans still are evolving, both biologically and culturally.

SUMMARY

This chapter explored the emergence of *Homo sapiens*, their biology, their geographic radiation, and aspects of their early culture that laid the foundation for their longevity.

1. The term *anatomically modern human* refers to the species *Homo sapiens*, the only living species of hominin.

2. It is widely accepted that the earliest hominins originated in Africa, but the origin of the species *H. sapiens* has been more controversial, with proponents of both an African origin and origins in Asia and other locations.

3. Fossil evidence and studies of variations in human DNA support an "Out of Africa" origin for *H. sapiens*.

4. The Replacement Model of modern human origins states that *H. sapiens* evolved in Africa about 200,000 years ago, radiated out of this area throughout the Old World, and replaced all separate species of *Homo* living in those places, including Neandertals.

5. The Regional Continuity Model of modern human origins states that modern human populations evolved simultaneously on their respective continents following the initial radiation of archaic humans out of Africa.

6. *H. sapiens* developed blade tool technology, a more efficient and economical means for making tools from stone.

7. *H. sapiens* lived in caves, rock shelters, and open spaces where they constructed shelters. They were a mobile people, probably moving seasonally to follow the availability of plants and animals throughout the year.

8. Upper Paleolithic humans probably used spoken language.

9. Burials provide evidence of ritual behavior and possible human sacrifice in early human cultures.

10. Upper Paleolithic art in the form of sculpted figures, ornamentation, inscribed tools, and cave paintings demonstrates that art played a role in the lives of early peoples as a means for acting out symbolic behavior and as a form of expression.

CONCLUSION

Human Evolution in a Changing World

In its 10 volumes, *The Prehistoric Earth* has traced the evolutionary history of life on Earth. The series has focused primarily on the natural forces that have affected the adaptation and speciation of vertebrates since the appearance of the small, basal fish *Myllokunmingia* in Asia 525 million years ago. Evolution is a continuing process that affects every form of life every day.

Humans are part of an interrelated biological web that includes all living organisms. Modern humans are part of a relatively recent thread of the vertebrate family tree. Whereas culture and the evolution of specialized adaptations have allowed humans to adapt to nearly any climate and geographic space on the planet, there also is little doubt that human expansion often has gravely affected the lives and the very existence of other organisms, from animals to plants and even to microorganisms, both on land and in the sea. Humans are equally affected, however, by the biological forces of evolution.

An aspect of human evolution that is sometimes misunderstood is that of race. Because all humans—*Homo sapiens*—are part of the same species and capable of interbreeding, there is no biological basis for considering differences in race as being synonymous with different species. Kottak defines race as a "geographically isolated subdivision of a species," with members of a given race sharing "distinctive physical characteristics," such as skin color, because of their common ancestry and "inheritance of the same genes." From the standpoint of a breeding population, races are not biologically distinct. The term *race* often is hijacked by political leaders, governments, and religious figures as a means to discredit and diminish the equality and rights of racial groups that are different from the majority group—a misrepresentation of science and morality that should be avoided at all costs. The importance of treating all people fairly is echoed by the American Anthropological Association in their statement on race:

> *How people have been accepted and treated within the context of a given society or culture has a direct impact on how they perform in that society. The "racial" world view was invented to assign some groups to perpetual low status, while other were permitted access to privilege, power, and wealth. . . . Given what we know about the capacity of normal humans to achieve and function within any culture, we conclude that present-day inequalities between so-called "racial" groups are not consequences of their biological inheritance but products of historical and contemporary social, economic, educational, and political circumstances.*

Differences in skin color are an interesting aspect of race. Skin color shared among different populations does not always indicate recent common ancestry. Dark-skinned native Australians and Africans developed dark skin without being related to one another. The answers to the questions of "why" and "how" lie in natural selection. Dark skin contains larger granules of the chemical melanin, a feature of skin that provides natural protection against the ultraviolet rays of the Sun. Setting aside factors related to human migration, people with ancestral roots in tropical habitats tend to have naturally darker skin than people outside the tropics. This naturally darker skin provides added protection against sunburn and disorders such as skin cancer. In colder northern or southern climates, where the Sun's rays are less intense, screening out ultraviolet rays is not as necessary as it is in the tropics. In these cooler climates, native peoples have fair skin to maximize absorption of the Sun's rays.

Recent human history and marriage between peoples of different races has naturally modified the biological distribution of skin color across the globe. The example of skin color is affected by both natural selection (the prehistoric geographic origin of a people) and the continuing history of human migration and ancestry that distributes skin color traits among populations through inheritance.

Humans still are evolving, but it is not likely that we will experience the kind of meaningful evolutionary changes—such as the rapid increase in brain size—observed in the rise of early hominins. The ability of such biological innovations to become fixed in the population requires a small, genetically unstable population in which a small change can be inherited and expanded, generation after generation.

Ian Tattersall points out that "for true innovations to arise and to become permanently incorporated into some component of the human population, it will be necessary for that population to become fragmented." Without small, isolated populations for natural selection to act on, it is unlikely that additional, large-scale biological changes can become part of the human gene pool. Human population has been expanding exponentially across the planet, making such isolation increasingly improbable.

This is not to say that humans are evolving less than before. Recall that evolution has no direction, has no particular pace, and has no expected outcome. It begins only at the level of the individual and in what that person is able to pass along to offspring in the way of inherited traits. Although large-scale biological changes to the human species—even the development of new human species—is now inhibited by the effects of population growth, the forces of evolution continue to affect people in many ways.

The development and spread of infectious diseases are connected intimately to changing environments, biology, and human behavior. The common cold is caused by a virus that can produce minor, nonlethal discomfort in millions of people every year. Deadly variants of the cold, such as Severe Acute Respiratory Syndrome— or SARS—can jump from animal populations to infect humans through molecular adaptation. SARS originated in such wild and domesticated animals in China as the civet cat, the dog, and the badger. The virus was able to jump to human populations when people in China began to butcher and eat infected animals. Once in the human population, SARS quickly evolved into a potentially lethal form that was spread as the common cold is spread.

SARS spread quickly from China to several other countries when unwary infected individuals traveled by airplane. It advanced suddenly to epidemic proportions in 2002 and 2003, killed more than 750 people, and then stabilized. Changes in human behavior— recognizing the illness, preventing the travel of infected individuals, and preventing the consumption of infected animals—helped bring SARS under control.

Every time an individual dies, the genetic variation represented by that person's individual DNA is removed from the pool of all human genes. Epidemic diseases such as influenza and even SARS have the potential to kill many thousands of people, thereby removing their unique genetic makeup from the mix. "After an epidemic is over," explains paleoanthropologist Agustin Fuentes, "the population that remains is genetically different from before (in terms of allele frequencies). Evolution has occurred."

Human behavior and technology continue to have enormous effects on the success of the human species. We are living in times of increasing diversity in human populations. The ability of people to travel freely across the globe allows individuals from all over the world to meet and reproduce. The mating of people with varying ancestry not only contributes to human diversity but also stabilizes the inherited factors that have become fixed in human populations. This is why, as Tattersall has explained, we cannot expect any dramatic morphological or even cognitive changes in the human race unless some part of the population becomes genetically isolated.

This is not to say that human evolution never again will undergo another dramatic change. While the inheritance of traits is a key factor in natural selection, so, too, is the ability of the organism to adjust to changes in its environment. One can find many examples in history of events that literally changed the rules of the game for life on Earth. For many species of organisms, the ability to survive and adapt to ever-changing environmental conditions ensures their longevity throughout the ages. Nature does not grant the survival of a species forever, however. There are times when even the hardiest of species fail to survive a gradual or sudden modification to their habitat. The fossil record confirms the fact that no species lasts forever. Every species eventually becomes extinct. Sometimes the cause of an extinction is so vast and so sudden that hundreds, perhaps thousands, of species are affected. A rapid change of this nature that wipes out significant numbers of species is called a *mass extinction.*

The spread of infectious disease is a recurring theme in human history. The Black Plague, which spread through Asia and Europe during the fourteenth century, may have killed as many as 25 million people in just a few years. The example of SARS, mentioned above, although an example of a disease that was quickly contained, reminds us that new strains of infectious disease can arise, evolve, and spread rapidly if left to do so without preventive measures.

HIV infection—infection by the human immunodeficiency virus—is another case in point. Although there still is no cure for AIDS—acquired immunodeficiency syndrome, the disease caused by the HIV virus—measures have been achieved to manage the health and longevity of people who have contracted the infection. Even so, the HIV virus is the widest known infectious disease in history. According to the Joint United Nations Programme on HIV/AIDS, an estimated 38.6 million people worldwide were living with HIV in 2005. In the same year, about 2.8 million people lost their lives to AIDS, and another 4.1 million became newly infected. This is the kind of pandemic that, if left unchecked, could change the course of evolution of human populations.

The role of technology both helps and hinders the occurrence and spread of deadly disease. Human mobility makes it likely that infectious diseases can spread far and wide more quickly than in the past. The technologies for curing disease, however, are not distributed equally to all segments of the world's population. While people living in industrialized nations have ready access to medical technology, those who live in less sophisticated societies may suffer more. The evolutionary effects of infectious disease may act more severely on one population than another, thus shifting the balance of the gene pool in favor of people of privilege.

The physiological features of modern humans are affected by cultural habits and eating behavior. Obesity in particular is a problem in many industrialized nations such as the United States, where people consume increasing quantities of processed and fast foods. The long-term effects of obesity and other nutritionally based maladies are unknown from an evolutionary standpoint. To some extent, however, they affect the ability of people to lead healthy lives and reproduce, thereby affecting the flow of genes within populations.

The course of human evolution also could be changed by a dramatic change to the world in which we live. Earth has undergone five major mass extinction events during the past 485 million years, the most famous being the demise of the last of the dinosaurs 65 million years ago. Such mass extinctions are caused by widespread geologic and climatic events that disturb habitats and interrupt the life cycles of existing organisms. Massive volcanic activity and even asteroid strikes have been implicated in several mass extinctions. Even humans, with all of their technology, will most likely be powerless to prevent such natural disasters in the future.

Some scientists claim that we currently are experiencing the time of the sixth great mass extinction, an event brought on the planet by humans themselves and by the stresses that modern technologies have placed on the environment, on natural resources, and on the companion species that share the world with people. Whether human technology will enable some members of the species to survive in the aftermath of such a disaster is a valid question, as is the question of how the forces of natural selection will act on the remaining populations of survivors, however fragmented.

The future of the human species will not necessarily be bleak, however. The forces of evolution and natural selection and the amazing ability of humans to adapt to the world around them result in successes as well as failures. There is no way to control which sort of result will dominate the other. We hope that this series, *The Prehistoric Earth,* has provided insight into the scientific method and the forces of evolution that affect the development of all organisms on the planet. Understanding the way that evolution works also acknowledges the kind of critical thinking and collaborative research that is an innate practice in science. Charles Darwin lauded the inner workings of science when he wrote:

> *"Nothing before had ever made me thoroughly realize, though I had read various scientific books, that science consists in grouping facts so that general laws or conclusions may be drawn from them."*

APPENDIX ONE:
GEOLOGIC TIME SCALE

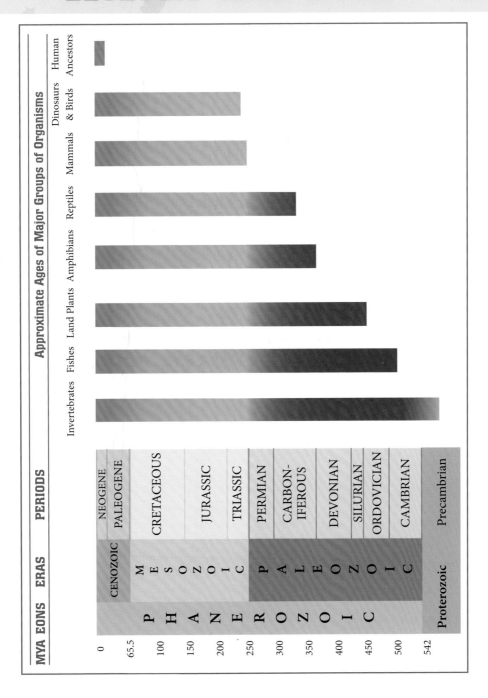

APPENDIX TWO: POSITIONAL TERMS

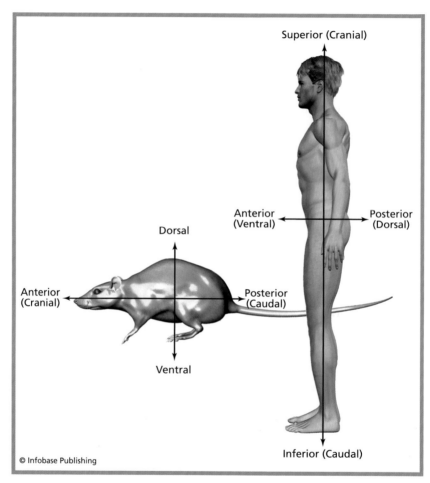

© Infobase Publishing

Positional terms used to describe vertebrate anatomy

GLOSSARY

adaptations   Anatomical, physiological, and behavioral changes that occur in an organism that enable it to survive environmental changes.

adaptive radiation   The diversification of a given population as it adapts to available ecological niches.

anatomically modern humans   Hominins of the species *Homo sapiens.*

anatomy   The basic biological systems of an animal, such as the skeletal and muscular systems.

anterior   Directional term meaning toward the head, or cranial, end of a vertebrate.

anthropoids   Higher primates (monkeys, apes, and humans).

anthropology   The study of human culture, evolution, and language.

australopithecines   Genera of ancestral humans that date primarily from the Pliocene Epoch.

bipedal (bipedalism)   Walking upright on two legs.

blade tool   An Upper Paleolithic toolmaking technology that used a stone flake twice as long as it was wide.

clade   A group of related organisms including all the descendants of a single common ancestor.

culture   The accumulation of acquired and learned behaviors shared by a population of organisms.

derived   Term used to describe a trait of an organism that is a departure from the most basal (ancestral) form.

diagnostic trait   A measurable feature in the morphology of a fossil that can be used to identify members of a given clade or taxon of extinct animal.

DNA   Deoxyribonucleic acid; the molecule that carries genetic code and that is found in every living cell of an organism. Genes are located on strands of DNA.

encephalization quotient (EQ)   Also known as a brain-to-body-mass ratio; a ratio that compares the actual brain mass of an animal with the expected brain mass of an animal of that size.

endocast   A cast made from the brain cavity inside the skull; an endocast shows the approximate size, shape, and connections associated with a brain.

evolution   The natural process by which species gradually change over time, controlled by changes to the genetic code—the DNA—of organisms and whether or not those changes enable an organism to survive in a given environment.

extant   Term used to describe an organism that is living today; not extinct.

extinction   The irreversible elimination of an entire species of organism because it cannot adapt effectively to changes in its environment.

foramen magnum   A hole in the bony base of the skull that marks the point of connection between the skull and the vertebral column.

forelimbs   The two front legs of a vertebrate.

fossil   Any physical trace or remains of prehistoric life.

gene   A portion of a DNA strand that controls a particular inherited trait.

gene pool   The combined genetic makeup of a species population.

genome   The complete genetic instructions embodied in the DNA of a species.

genus (plural: genera)   A taxonomic name entity for one or more closely related organisms that is divided into species; names of organisms, such as *Tyrannosaurus rex*, are composed of two parts, the genus name (first) and the species name (second).

glacial   Term used to describe a period of glaciation, or ice-sheet formation.

hominin   (alternatively: hominid) Fossil and living humans.

Homo sapiens   Modern human species.

hunter-gatherers   Term used to describe a population that relies on the availability of natural plant and animal resources for its subsistence.

interglacial   Term used to describe a period between glaciations when ice sheets retreat.

material culture   Objects and artifacts left by hominin cultures and found in the fossil record.

metabolism   (adjective: metabolic) The combination of all biochemical processes that take place in an organism to keep it alive.

morphological   Pertaining to the body form and structure of an organism.

natural selection   One of Darwin's observations regarding the way in which evolution works; given the complex and changing conditions under which life exists, those individuals with the combination of inherited traits best suited to a particular environment will survive and reproduce while others will not.

neural   Pertaining to the nerves or nervous system; term used to describe nerves and associated connections to the brain.

New World   The Americas.

Old World   Africa, Asia, and Europe.

paleoanthropologist   Scientist who studies human origins using fossils as a key source of information.

paleontologist   Scientist who studies prehistoric life, often using fossils.

phylogeny   The family tree of a group of related organisms based on shared, inherited traits.

population   Members of the same species that live in a particular area.

postcranial   "Behind the head"; term generally used to refer to the portion of the vertebrate skeleton other than the head.

posterior   Directional term meaning toward the tail end; also known as the caudal end.

predator   Animal that actively seeks, kills, and feeds on other animals.

prognathism   Having a jaw that juts forward from the face; a primitive trait of hominin anatomy.

robust   Having a relatively larger, more muscular body.

sagittal crest   A bony ridge on top of the skull.

sedimentary   Word used to describe layers of rock deposited over time; sedimentary rock may contain fossils.

sexual dimorphism   Variation between males and females of a species.

speciation   The evolution of new species.

species   In classification, the most basic biological unit of living organisms; members of a species can interbreed and produce fertile offspring.

taxon   (plural: taxa) In classification, a single kind of organism; the word *taxa* describes a group of related organisms.

theory   A comprehensive, testable explanation about some aspect of the natural world that is backed by an extensive body of facts over time.

transitional   Representing one step in the many stages that exist as a species evolves.

CHAPTER BIBLIOGRAPHY

Preface

Wilford, John Noble. "When No One Read, Who Started to Write?" *New York Times* (April, 6, 1999). Available online. URL: http://query. nytimes.com/gst/fullpage.html?res=9B01EFD61139F935A35757C0A9 6F958260. Accessed May 21, 2008.

Chapter 1 – Early Hominins and the Emergence of the Genus *Homo*

Alemseged, Zeresenay, Fred Spoor, William H. Kimbel, René Bobe, Denis Geraads, Denné Reed, and Jonathan G. Wynn. "A Juvenile Early Hominin Skeleton from Dikika, Ethiopia." *Nature* 443 (September 21, 2006): 296–301.

Alexander, Richard D. "How Did Humans Evolve?" Museum of Zoology, University of Michigan, *Special Publication No. 1* (1990): 1–38.

Brunet, Michel, Franck Guy, David Pilbeam, Daniel E. Lieberman, Andossa Likius, Hassane T. Mackaye, Marcia S. Ponce de León, Christoph P.E. Zollikofer, and Patrick Vignaud. "New Material of the Earliest Hominid from the Upper Miocene of Chad." *Nature* 434 (April 7, 2005): 752–755.

Carroll, Sean B. "Genetics and the Making of *Homo sapiens*." *Nature* 422 (April 24, 2003): 849–857.

Fagan, Brian. "Aping the Apes." Available online. URL: http://www. mc.maricopa.edu/~reffland/anthropology/anthro2003/origins/ hominid_journey/apingtheapes.html. Accessed May 21, 2008.

Fuentes, Agustin. *Core Concepts in Biological Anthropology*. New York: McGraw-Hill, 2007.

Haviland, William A., Harald E.L. Prins, Dana Walrath, and Bunny McBride. *Anthropology: The Human Challenge*, 12th ed. New York: Wadsworth, 2008.

Hopkin, Michael. "Fossil Find Is Oldest European Yet: Spanish jawbone is earliest human remains from Western Europe." *News@Nature*,

March 26, 2008. Available online. URL: http://www.nature.com/news/2008/080326/full/news.2008.691.html. Accessed May 21, 2008.

Jurmain, Robert, Lynn Kilgore, Wenda Trevathan. *Introduction to Physical Anthropology*, 10th ed. New York: Wadsworth, 2005.

Kottak, Conrad Phillip. *Anthropology: The Exploration of Human Diversity*, 12th ed. New York: McGraw-Hill, 2008.

Lee, S.-H. "Patterns of size sexual dimorphism in *Australopithecus afarensis*: Another look." *HOMO—Journal of Comparative Human Biology*. Vol. 56, No. 3 (December 8, 2005): 219–232.

Lordkipanidze, David, Tea Jashashvili, Abesalom Vekua, Marcia S. Ponce de León, Christoph P.E. Zollikofer, G. Philip Rightmire, Herman Pontzer, Reid Ferring, Oriol Oms, MarthaTappen, Maia Bukhsianidze, Jordi Agusti, Ralf Kahlke, Gocha Kiladze, Bienvenido Martinez-Navarro, Alexander Mouskhelishvili, Medea Nioradze, and Lorenzo Rook. "Postcranial Evidence from Early *Homo* from Dmanisi, Georgia." *Nature* 449, no. 7146 (September 20, 2007): 306–310.

Potts, Richard. "Variability in Hominid Evolution." *Evolutionary Anthropology* 7, no. 3 (1998): 81–96.

Spoor, F., M.G. Leakey, P.N. Gathogo, F.H. Brown, S.C. Antón, I. McDougall, C. Kiarie, F.K. Manthi, and L.N. Leakey. "Implications of New Early *Homo* Fossils from Ileret, East of Lake Turkana, Kenya." *Nature* 448 (August 9, 2007): 688–691.

Wilson, A.C. and V.M. Sarich. "A Molecular Time Scale for Human Evolution." *Proceedings of the National Academy of Sciences of the United States* 69 (1969): 1088–1093.

Wolpoff, Milford H., Brigitte Senut, Martine Pickford, and John Hawks. "*Sahelanthropus* or *Sahelpithecus*?" *Nature* 419 (October 10, 2002): 581–582.

Wood, Bernard, and Nicholas Lonergan. "The hominin fossil record: Taxa, grades and clades." *Journal of Anatomy*, 212 (2008): 354–376.

Wood, Bernard. "The History of the Genus *Homo*." *Human Evolution*, 15, nos. 1–2 (2000): 39–49.

Chapter 2 – Archaic *Homo* Species

Brain, C.K., and A. Sillent. "Evidence from the Swartkrans Cave for the Earliest Use of Fire." *Nature* 336 (December 1, 1988): 464–466.

Carbonell, Eudald, José M. Bermúdez de Castro, Josep M. Parés, Alfredo Pérez-Gonzalez, Gloria Cuenca-Bescós, Andreu Ollé,

Marina Mosquera, Rosa Huguet, Jan van der Made, Antonio Rosas, Robert Sala, Josep Vallverdú, Nuria García, Darry E. Granger, María Martinón-Torres, Xosé P. Rodríguez, Greg M. Stock, Josep M. Vergés, Ethel Allué, Francesc Burjachs, Isabel Cáceres, Antoni Canals, Alfonso Benito, Carlos Díez, Marina Lozano, Ana Mateos, Marta Navazo, Jesús Rodríguez, Jordi Rosell, and Juan L. Arsuaga. "The First Hominin of Europe." *Nature* 452 (March 27, 2008): 465–470.

Chen, Tie-Mei, Quan Yang, Yan-Qiu Hu, Wen-Bo Bao and Tian-Yuan Li. "ESR Dating of Tooth Enamel from Yunxian *Homo erectus* Site, China." *Quaternary Science Reviews* 16, nos. 3–5 (1997): 455–458.

Dalton, Rex. "Looking for the Ancestors." *Nature* 434 (March 24, 2005): 432–434.

Latimer, B.M., and C.O. Lovejoy. "Hallucal Tarsometatarsal Joint in *Australopithecus afarensis*." *American Journal of Physical Anthropology* 82, no. 2 (1990): 125–133.

Lee, S.-H. "Patterns of Size Sexual Dimorphism in *Australopithecus afarensis*: Another look." *HOMO—Journal of Comparative Human Biology* 56 (2005): 219–232.

Neumann, Nadja. "Earliest Fire Sheds Light on Hominids: Ancient hearths unveiled as nearly 800 millennia old." *News@Nature*, April 30, 2004. Available online. URL: http://www.nature.com/news/2004/040426/full/news040426–16.html. Accessed May 21, 2008.

Park, Michael Alan. *Biological Anthropology*, 5th ed. New York: McGraw-Hill, 2008.

Potts, Richard, Anna K. Behrensmeyer, and Peter Ditchfield. "Paleolandscape Variation and Early Pleistocene Hominid Activities: Members 1 and 7, Olorgesailie Formation, Kenya." *Journal of Human Evolution* 37 (1999): 747–788.

Pyne, Stephen J. *Fire: A Brief History*. London: British Museum Press, 2001.

Reno, Philip L., Richard S. Meindl, Melanie A. McCollum, and C. Owen Lovejoy. "Sexual Dimorphism in *Australopithecus afarensis* Was Similar to that of Modern Humans." *Proceedings of the National Academy of Sciences of the United States* 100 (August 5, 2003): 9404–9409.

Robson, Shannen L., and Bernard Wood. "Hominin Life History: Reconstruction and Evolution." *Journal of Anatomy* 212 (2008): 394–425.

Shipman, Pat. *The Man Who Found the Missing Link: Eugène Dubois and His Lifelong Quest to Prove Darwin Right*. New York: Simon and Schuster, 2001.

Stein, Philip L., and Bruce M. Rowe. *Physical Anthropology*, 8th ed. New York: McGraw-Hill, 2003.

Tattersall, Ian. *The Monkey in the Mirror*. New York: Harcourt, 2002.

Tianyuan, Li and Dennis A. Etler. "New Middle Pleistocene Hominid Crania from Yunxian in China." *Nature* 357 (June 4, 1992): 404–407.

Wood, Bernard, and Mark Collard. "The Changing Face of Genus *Homo*." *Evolutionary Anthropology* 8, no. 6 (1999): 195–207

Wood, Bernard. "A Precious Little Bundle." *Nature* 443 (September 21, 2006): 278–281.

Woodward, A. Smith. "Note on the Piltdown Man (Eoanthropus Dawsoni)." *Geological Magazine,* October 1913.

Chapter 3 – Premodern Humans of the Genus *Homo*

Bird, M.I., and L.K. Fifield. "Archaeology and Age of a New Hominin from Flores in Eastern Indonesia." *Nature* 431 (October 28, 2004): 1087–1091.

Broen, P., T. Sutikna, M.J. Morwood, R.P. Soejono, E. Jatmiko, Wayhu Saptomo, and Rokus Awe Due. "A New Small-bodied Hominin from the Late Pleistocene of Flores, Indonesia." *Nature* 431 (October 28, 2004): 1055–1061.

Dalton, Rex. "Hobbit Was 'a Cretin.' " *News@Nature*, March 4, 2008. Available online. URL: http://www.nature.com/news/2008/080304/full/news.2008.643.html. Accessed May 21, 2008.

Dalton, Rex. "Little Lady of Flores Forces Rethink of Human Evolution." *Nature* 431 (October 28, 2004): 1029.

Dalton, Rex. "More Evidence for Hobbit Unearthed as Diggers Are Refused Access to Cave." *Nature* 437 (October 13, 2005): 934–935.

Delson, Eric, Ian Tattersall, and John A. Van Couvering. *Encyclopedia of Human Evolution and Prehistory*, 2nd ed. New York: Routledge, 1999.

Enard, Wolfgang, Molly Przeworski, Simon E. Fisher, Cecilia S.L. Lai, Victor Wiebe, Takashi Kitano, Anthony P. Monaco, and Svante Pääbo. "Molecular Evolution of FOXP2, a Gene Involved in Speech and Language." *Nature* 418 (August 22, 2002): 869–872.

Finlayson, Clive, Francisco Giles Pacheco, Joaquín Rodríguez-Vidal, Darren A. Fa, José María Gutierrez López, Antonio Santiago Pérez, Geraldine Finlayson, Ethel Allue, Javier Baena Preysler, Isabel Cáceres, José S. Carrión, Yolanda Fernández Jalvo, Christopher P. Gleed-Owen, Francisco J. Jimenez Espejo, Pilar López, José Antonio López Sáez, José Antonio Riquelme Cantal, Antonio Sánchez

Marco, Francisco Giles Guzman, Kimberly Brown, Noemí Fuentes, Claire A. Valarino, Antonio Villalpando, Christopher B. Stringer, Francisca Martinez Ruiz, and Tatsuhiko Sakamoto. "Late Survival of Neanderthals at the Southernmost Extreme of Europe." *Nature* 443 (October 19, 2006): 330–336.

Foley, R.A., and M. Mirazón Lahr. "The Base Nature of Neanderthals." *Heredity* 98 (2007): 187–188.

Fuentes, Agustin. *Core Concepts in Biological Anthropology*. New York: McGraw-Hill, 2007.

Gordon, Adam D., Lisa Nevell, and Bernard Wood. "The *Homo floresiensis* cranium (LB1): Size, scaling, and early *Homo* affinities." *Proceedings of the National Academy of Sciences of the United States* 105, no. 12 (March 25, 2008): 4650–4655.

Green, Richard E., Johannes Krause, Susan E. Ptak, Adrian W. Briggs, Michael T. Ronan, Jan F. Simons, Lei Du, Michael Egholm, Jonathan M. Rothberg, Maja Paunovic, and Svante Pøaøabo. "Analysis of One Million Base Pairs of Neanderthal DNA." *Nature* 444 (November 16, 2006): 330–336.

Haviland, William A., Harald E.L. Prins, Dana Walrath, and Bunny McBride. *Anthropology: The Human Challenge*, 12th ed. New York: Wadsworth, 2008.

Hopkin, Michael. "Old Tools Shed Light on Hobbit Origins." *Nature* 441 (June 1, 2006): 559.

Hopkin, Michael. "The Flores Find." *News@Nature*, October 27, 2004. Available online. URL: http://www.nature.com/news/2004/041025/full/news041025-4.html. Accessed May 21, 2008.

Hopkin, Michael. "Wrist Bones Bolster Hobbit Status." *News@Nature*, September 20, 2007. Available online. URL: http://www.nature.com/news/2007/070920/full/news070917-8.html. Accessed May 21, 2008.

Jurmain, Robert, Lynn Kilgore, Wenda Trevathan. *Introduction to Physical Anthropology*, 10th ed. New York: Wadsworth, 2005.

Kottak, Conrad Phillip. *Anthropology: The Exploration of Human Diversity*, 12th ed. New York: McGraw-Hill, 2008.

Krause, Johannes, Carles Lalueza-Fox, Ludovic Orlando, Wolfgang Enard, Richard E. Green, Hernán A. Burbano, Jean-Jacques Hublin, Catherine Hänni, Javier Fortea, Marco de la Rasilla, Jaume Bertranpetit, Antonio Rosas, and Svante Pääbo. "The Derived FOXP2 Variant of Modern Humans Was Shared with Neandertals." *Current Biology* 17:21 (November 6, 2007): 1908–1912.

Krings, Matthias, Anne Stone, Ralf W. Schmitz, Heike Krainitzki, Mark Stoneking, and Svante Pääbo. "Neandertal DNA Sequences and the Origin of Modern Humans." *Cell* 90 (July 11, 1997): 19–30.

Lahr, Marta Mirazón, and Robert Foley. "Human Evolution Writ Small." *Nature* 431 (October 28, 2004): 1043–1044.

Morwood, M.J., R.P. Soejono, R.G. Roberts, T. Sutikna, C.S.M. Turney, K.E. Westaway, W.J. Rink, J.-X. Zhao, G.D. van den Bergh, Rokus Awe Due, D.R. Hobbs, M.W. Moore, M. I. Bird, and L. K. Fifield. "Archaeology and Age of a New Hominin from Flores in Eastern Indonesia." *Nature* 431 (October 28, 2004): 1087–1091.

Noonan, James P., Graham Coop, Sridhar Kudaravalli, Doug Smith, Johannes Krause, Joe Alessi, Feng Chen, Darren Platt, Svante Pääbo, Jonathan K. Pritchard, and Edward M. Rubin. "Sequencing and Analysis of Neanderthal Genomic DNA." *Science* 314, no. 5802 (November 17, 2006): 1113–1118.

Park, Michael Alan, editor. *Biological Anthropology: An Introductory Reader*, 5th ed. New York: McGraw-Hill, 2008.

Park, Michael Alan. *Biological Anthropology*, 5th ed. New York: McGraw-Hill, 2008.

Patou-Mathis, Maryléne. "Neanderthal Subsistence Behaviours in Europe." *International Journal of Osteoarchaeology* 10, no. 5 (October 11, 2000): 379–395.

Schmid, Randolph E. "Researchers May Remake Neanderthal DNA." *Physorg.com/Associated Press*, June 26, 2007. Available online. URL: http://www.physorg.com/news102055359.html. Accessed May 21, 2008.

Stein, Philip L., and Bruce M. Rowe. *Physical Anthropology*, 8th ed. New York: McGraw-Hill, 2003.

Stringer, Chris. "A Stranger from Flores." *News@Nature*, October 27, 2004. Available online. URL: http://www.nature.com/news/2004/041025/full/news041025-3.html. Accessed May 21, 2008.

Tattersall, Ian. *The Monkey in the Mirror*. New York: Harcourt, 2002.

Thieme, Hartmut. "Lower Palaeolithic Hunting Spears from Germany." *Nature* 385 (February 27, 1997): 807–80.

Chapter 4 – The Emergence of Modern Humans— *Homo sapiens*

Cavalli-Sforza, L. Luca, and Marcus W. Feldman. "The Application of Molecular Genetic Approaches to the Study of Human Evolution." *Nature Genetics* 33 (2003): 266–275.

Einwögerer, Thomas, Herwig Friesinger, Marc Händel, Christine Neugebauer-Maresch, Ulrich Simon, and Maria Teschler-Nicola. "Upper Palaeolithic Infant Burials." *Nature* 444 (November 16, 2006): 285.

Finlayson, Clive. "Biogeography and Evolution of the Genus *Homo*." *Trends in Ecology and Evolution* 20, no. 8 (August 2005): 457–463.

Fuentes, Agustin. *Core Concepts in Biological Anthropology*. New York: McGraw-Hill, 2007.

Gaudzinski, Sabine, and Wil Roebroeks. "Reindeer Hunting at the Middle Palaeolithic Site Salzgitter Lebenstedt, Northern Germany." *Journal of Human Evolution* 38, no. 4 (April 2000): 497–521.

Haviland, William A., Harald E.L. Prins, Dana Walrath, and Bunny McBride. *Anthropology: The Human Challenge*, 12th ed. New York: Wadsworth, 2008.

Hayden, Brian. "Research and Development in the Stone Age: Technological Transitions among Hunter-Gatherers." *Current Anthropology* 22, no. 5 (October 1981).

Jurmain, Robert, Lynn Kilgore, and Wenda Trevathan. *Introduction to Physical Anthropology*, 10th ed. New York: Wadsworth, 2005.

Kottak, Conrad Phillip. *Anthropology: The Exploration of Human Diversity*, 12th ed. New York: McGraw-Hill, 2008.

Lieberman, Daniel E. "Homing in on Early *Homo*." *Nature* 449 (September 20, 2007): 291–292.

Owen, James. "Human Sacrifice Clues Found in European Stone Age Burials." *National Geographic News*, May 30, 2007. Available online. URL: http://news.nationalgeographic.com/news/2007/05/070530-sacrifice-burial.html. Accessed May 21, 2008.

Park, Michael Alan, editor. *Biological Anthropology: An Introductory Reader*, 5th ed. New York: McGraw-Hill, 2008.

Park, Michael Alan. *Biological Anthropology*, 5th ed. New York: McGraw-Hill, 2008.

Relethford, J.H. *Genetics and the Search for Modern Human Origins*. New York, Wiley, 2001.

Shreeve, James. *The Neandertal Enigma: Solving the Mystery of Modern Human Origins*. New York: William Morrow, 1995.

Stein, Philip L., and Bruce M. Rowe. *Physical Anthropology*, 8th ed. New York: McGraw-Hill, 2003.

Stringer C.B., Andrews, P. "Genetic and Fossil Evidence for the Origin of Modern Humans." *Science* 239 (1988): 1263–1268.

Templeton, Alan R. "Out of Africa Again and Again." *Nature* 416 (March 7, 2002): 45–51.

Underhill, P. *et al.* "The Phylogeography of Y Chromosome Binary Haplotypes and the Origins of Modern Human Populations." *Annals of Human Genetics* 65 (2001): 43–62.

Wolpoff, M.H. "Multiregional Evolution: The fossil alternative to Eden." In *The Human Revolution: Behavioural and Biological Perspectives on the Origins of Modern Humans.* P. Mellar and C. Stringer, editors. Princeton: Princeton University Press, 1989: 62–108.

Wood, Bernard, and Mark Collard. "The Human Genus." *Science* 284, no. 5411 (April 2, 1999): 65–71.

Conclusion – Human Evolution in a Changing World

Darwin, Francis, ed. *The Life and Letters of Charles Darwin, Including an Autobiographical Chapter,* Vol. 1. London: John Murray, 1887: 75.

Fuentes, Agustin. *Core Concepts in Biological Anthropology.* New York: McGraw-Hill, 2007.

Joint United Nations Programme on HIV/AIDS (2006). "Overview of the Global AIDS epidemic," 2006 Report on the global AIDS epidemic. Available online. URL: http://data.unaids.org/pub/GlobalReport/2006/2006_GR_CH02_en.pdf. Accessed June 1, 2008.

National Geographic. "Plague." Available online. URL: http://science.nationalgeographic.com/science/health-and-human-body/human-diseases/plague-article.html. Accessed June 1, 2008.

Tattersall, Ian. *The Monkey in the Mirror.* New York: Harcourt, 2002.

FURTHER READING

Benton, Michael. *Vertebrate Paleontology*, 3rd ed. Oxford: Blackwell Publishing, 2005.

Ellis, Richard. *No Turning Back: The Life and Death of Animal Species*. New York: Harper Collins, 2004.

Ember, Carol R., Melvin Ember, and Peter N. Peregrine. *Anthropology*, 11th ed. Upper Saddle River, NJ: Prentice Hall, 2005.

Fleagle, John G. *Primate Adaptation & Evolution*. New York: Academic Press, 1988.

Fuentes, Agustin. *Core Concepts in Biological Anthropology*. New York: McGraw-Hill, 2007.

Haviland, William A., Harald E.L. Prins, Dana Walrath, and Bunny McBride. *Anthropology: The Human Challenge*, 12th ed. New York: Wadsworth, 2008.

Jolly, Clifford J., and Randall White. *Physical Anthropology and Archaeology*, 5th ed. New York: McGraw-Hill, 1995.

Jurmain, Robert, Lynn Kilgore, Wenda Trevathan. *Introduction to Physical Anthropology*, 10th ed. New York: Wadsworth, 2005.

Kemp, T.S. *The Origin and Evolution of Mammals*. Oxford: Oxford University Press, 2005.

Kottak, Conrad Phillip. *Anthropology: The Exploration of Human Diversity*, 12th ed. New York: McGraw-Hill, 2008.

Miller, Barbara D., and Bernard Wood. *Anthropology*. New York: Allyn and Bacon, 2006.

Park, Michael Alan, ed. *Biological Anthropology: An Introductory Reader*, 5th ed. New York: McGraw-Hill, 2008.

Park, Michael Alan. *Biological Anthropology*, 5th ed. New York: McGraw-Hill, 2008.

Prothero, Donald R. *After the Dinosaurs: The Age of Mammals*. Bloomington: Indiana University Press, 2006.

Raven, Peter H., George B. Johnson, Jonathan B. Losos, and Susan R. Singer. *Biology*, 7th ed. New York: McGraw-Hill, 2005.

Stanford, Craig, John S. Allen, and Susan C. Antón. *Biological Anthropology*. Upper Saddle River, NJ: Prentice Hall, 2006.

Stein, Philip L., and Bruce M. Rowe. *Physical Anthropology*, 8th ed. New York: McGraw-Hill, 2003.

Stokstad, Marilyn. *Art History*, 3rd ed. Upper Saddle River, NJ: Prentice Hall, 2008.

Tattersall, Ian. *The Monkey in the Mirror*. New York: Harcourt, 2002.

Turner, Alan, and Mauricio Anton. *Evolving Eden*. New York: Columbia University Press, 2004.

Wallace, D.R. *Beasts of Eden*. Berkeley: University of California Press, 2004.

Wolpoff, Milford H. *Paleoanthropology*, 2nd ed. New York: McGraw-Hill, 1999.

Web Sites

Archaeology.Info: Human Ancestry

A public-education project organized by a team of anthropology fieldworkers. The site houses an excellent gallery of photos of fossil hominin skulls.

http://www.archaeologyinfo.com/evolution.htm

BBC: Human Beginnings

A collection of text and video content related to the evolution of humans, sponsored by the British Broadcasting Corporation.

http://www.bbc.co.uk/sn/prehistoric_life/human/

Hominid Journey, The

An excellent interactive timeline of hominin evolution sponsored by Mesa Community College in Mesa, Arizona. The site also includes a wealth of information about biological anthropology and primate evolution.

http://www.mc.maricopa.edu/~reffland/anthropology/anthro2003/origins/hominid_journey/central.html

International Commission on Stratigraphy. International Stratigraphic Chart

Downloadable geologic time scales provided by the International Commission on Stratigraphy.

http://www.stratigraphy.org/cheu.pdf

Maddison, D.R., and K.-S. Schulz. The Tree of Life Web Project

The Tree of Life Web Project is a meticulously designed view of life-forms based on their phylogenetic (evolutionary) connections. It is hosted by the University of Arizona College of Agriculture and Life Sciences and the University of Arizona Library.

http://tolweb.org/tree/phylogeny.html

National Museums of Kenya

Guide to museums in Kenya, many of which house important fossils of ancestral humans from East Africa.

http://www.museums.or.ke/

National Primate Research Center, University of Wisconsin, Primate Info Net

An excellent resource for scientific information about living primates. Includes fact sheets about different species and an audio-visual library of primate vocalizations and research video.

http://pin.primate.wisc.edu/index.html

Public Broadcasting Service. Evolution Library: Evidence for Evolution

This resource outlines the extensive evidence in support of both the fact and theory of evolution, basing its approach on studies of the fossil record, molecular sequences, and comparative anatomy.

http://www.pbs.org/wgbh/evolution/library/04/

Scotese, Christopher R. Paleomap Project

A valuable source of continental maps showing the positioning of Earth's continents over the course of geologic time.

http://www.scotese.com/

SOMSO Modelle, Reconstructions of Primate and Hominin Skulls

This is the Web site of a commercial maker of scientifically accurate skulls and skeletal bones of extinct apes and hominins. This link features a gallery of these images.

http://www.somso.de/index.htm?f=english/anatomie/stammesgeschichte.htm

Teaching About Evolution and the Nature of Science

This educational resource designed for high school science teachers provides background, research ideas, and facts regarding human evolution as defined by the National Research Council.

http://www.nap.edu/html/evolution98/evol6-d.html

University of California Museum of Paleontology. History of Evolutionary Thought

A tutorial about the thinkers who founded the modern science of evolutionary biology.

http://www.ucmp.berkeley.edu/history/evothought.html

University of Michigan Museum of Anthropology

The Museum of Anthropology is an internationally recognized center for anthropological and archaeological research. This Web site contains information about faculty research and the museum's organization and offers selected images from the museum's collections.

http://www.lsa.umich.edu/umma/

Picture Credits

INDEX

ABOUT THE AUTHOR

THOM HOLMES is a writer specializing in natural history subjects and dinosaurs. He is noted for his expertise on the early history of dinosaur science in America. He was the publications director of *The Dinosaur Society* for six years (1991–1997) and the editor of its newsletter, *Dino Times*, the world's only monthly publication devoted to news about dinosaur discoveries. It was through the Society and his work with the Academy of Natural Sciences in Philadelphia that Thom developed widespread contacts and working relationships with paleontologists and paleo-artists throughout the world.

Thom's published works include *Fossil Feud: The Rivalry of America's First Dinosaur Hunters* (Silver Burdett Press, September, 1997); *The Dinosaur Library* (Enslow, *2001–2002*); *Duel of the Dinosaur Hunters* (Pearson Education, *2002*); *Fossil Feud: The First American Dinosaur Hunters* (Silver Burdett/Julian Messner, 1997). His many honors and awards include the National Science Teachers Association's *Outstanding Science Book of 1998*, VOYA's 1997 Nonfiction Honor List, an Orbis Pictus Honor, and the Chicago Public Library Association's *"Best of the Best"* in science books for young people.

Thom did undergraduate work in geology and studied paleontology through his role as a staff educator with the Academy of Natural Sciences in Philadelphia. He is a regular participant in field exploration, with two recent expeditions to Patagonia in association with Canadian, American, and Argentinian universities.